Shifting Paradigms

Essays on Art & Culture

Essential Essays Series 76

Guernica Editions Inc. acknowledges the support of
the Canada Council for the Arts and the Ontario Arts Council.
The Ontario Arts Council is an agency of the Government of Ontario.
We acknowledge the financial support of the Government of Canada

Shifting Paradigms

Essays on Art & Culture

Ewan Whyte

GUERNICA
EDITIONS

TORONTO • CHICAGO • BUFFALO • LANCASTER (U.K.)
2021

Guernica Founder: Antonio D'Alfonso

Michael Mirolla, editor
Cover layout and typesetting: Rafael Chimicatti
Cover and interior design: David Moratto
Guernica Editions Inc.
287 Templemead Drive, Hamilton (ON), Canada L8W 2W4
2250 Military Road, Tonawanda, N.Y. 14150-6000 U.S.A.
www.guernicaeditions.com

Distributors:
Independent Publishers Group (IPG)
600 North Pulaski Road, Chicago IL 60624
University of Toronto Press Distribution (UTP)
5201 Dufferin Street, Toronto (ON), Canada M3H 5T8
Gazelle Book Services, White Cross Mills
High Town, Lancaster LA1 4XS U.K.

First edition.
Printed in Canada.

Legal Deposit—Third Quarter
Library of Congress Catalog Card Number: 2020934508
Library and Archives Canada Cataloguing in Publication
Title: Shifting paradigms : essays on art & culture / Ewan Whyte.
Names: Whyte, Ewan, author.
Series: Essential essays series ; 76.
Description: 1st edition. | Series statement: Essential essays series ; 76
Identifiers: Canadiana (print) 2020020761X | Canadiana (ebook) 20200207628
ISBN 9781771835633 (softcover) | ISBN 9781771835640 (EPUB)
ISBN 9781771835657 (Kindle)
Subjects: LCSH: Art, Canadian. | LCSH: Artists—Canada.
LCSH: Authors, Canadian. | LCGFT: Essays.
Classification: LCC NX513.A1 W49 2020 | DDC 709.71—dc23

Contents

For Marcus

Death Denied

Damien Hirst (2008)

Death Denied (2008) - photo by Agent 001 WC CC-BY-SA

A giant human killing shark is the stuff of nightmares, but in formaldehyde in an art gallery it is art. Terrifying and hilarious, this prospect of terror has become a collective fear for most of us. Who has not had a dream where they were attacked by or eaten by a shark? The current media have presented enough instances of shark attacks that we're all conscious of it when we go swimming.

Even if we know it is ridiculous, we can still tease people. Or if you are a jerk of a kid, terrify other children by humming shark attack sounds or references to them in film. The prospect of this kind of death is a constructed terror even if the likelihood of death is laughably low, unless you happen to be a careless spear-fisher in the South China sea.

It is a confrontation of death, which we all fear. It reminds me of Ernest Becker's once famous book the *Denial of Death* where he lists off psychological ways we hide this fear from our conscious selves. Going to the toilet being a daily one. This brings it home to us and we look at the prospect of death with a close lens and it is, among other things, a kind of way to deny it in the spectacle of distance. If it is art, we can handle it. It has something resembling a frame around it.

This is art though. To go to an art gallery to see a shark and know that, in its environment, this dreaded fish is the top of the food chain and we are not—at least while we are in the ocean in a wild gadgetless state.

Hirst spent about £50,000 (about $69,000 Canadian) to have a fisherman catch the shark, and then have it prepared in formaldehyde for display. Hirst said of the prospective shark that he wanted it, "big enough to eat you."

This is a work anyone could get something out of, from a child preferring being at the zoo to the snottiest social art climber. It is a bit of an inspired work on many levels.

Even prospective protesters of Hirst killing a nearly endangered fish for a work of art could be presented as being both provocative and twistedly funny.[1] The prospect of potential protesters of these series of shark works holding signs and singing the YouTube popular song "Baby Shark" beside the exhibit would be, for a moment, hilarity. There are circuses around Hirst's work. These have had their detractors but he continues to create and to shock, and also to delight. As time goes on, perhaps Robert Hughes, for all his disgust, was accidently promoting Hirst, in another of his shark works:

> In a speech at the Royal Academy in 2004, art critic Robert Hughes used *The Physical Impossibility of Death in the Mind of Someone Living* as a prime example of how the international art market at the time was a "cultural obscenity." ("Art Market a 'cultural obscenity'," *The Guardian*, 3 June 2004).

Death Denied (2008) - photo by Agent 001 WC CC-BY-SA

---

1. The World Conservation Union (IUCN) lists the tiger shark as "Near Threatened" throughout its range. However, they do not face a high risk of extinction at the present time.

An earlier version did decay due to bleach being added to the mixture. The shark skin was then placed on a fiberglass mould. Hirst reportedly commented that: "It didn't look as frightening ... You could tell it wasn't real. It had no weight."

A new shark was prepared, and it looks like we are seeing death.

One of Hirst's shark works sold for over £9.6 ($13.6) million at Sotheby's in September, 2008.

Clown or not, he certainly gets a reaction.

Anish Kapoor

In the National Gallery of Canada

In the early nineties in the contemporary wing of the National gallery of Canada I stumbled on the young Anish Kapoor setting up an exhibit of his work. I was with several other art students. The gallery was mostly empty. Kapoor was working on a temporary installation of his work on the floor. He spoke to us as we were watching him organize his work in the large space. None of us realized he was such an art star or where he was headed in the art world, fresh off his Turner Prize. We were about to be exposed to his art of listening.

He was friendly and, surprisingly to us, interested in what a few young random art students thought of his art and how we might interact with his work. I asked him about structure in his work, and possible geometrical patterns in his floor construction. He surprised by describing it as an entirely intuitive creation process, laying out what looked like blue felt covered rocks in an arrangement on the floor. It appeared to be a requirement of his to make an installation that would fill the large space to accompany a few his permanent works that were the main part of the exhibit.

Kapoor was very interested in the art experience of others, not just in transmitting or expressing an idea or an aesthetic of his own. I had recently several long conversations with an established older artist about structure in art in general. He had very clear ideas where he was headed with each of his works. Kapoor explained the installation. He had time for questions about Leonardo Da Vinci's famous phrase which the older artist delighted in: "Those who practice art without order are like those who get on a ship without a rudder and set sail." He appeared amused though not condescending. He expressed circuitously that he thought there are several ways to arrive at a work of art.

He then asked what we thought of the other works being readied for display. One by one he asked each of us what we thought of each work. He had me stand in the middle of his work "Three Witches" and asked what I thought and what I felt. (His interest in scapegoating seemed a difficult thing to capture in sculpture). I said, with the honestly of youth, that it seemed the title of his work rather than the sculpture (his seemed to have guessed the response before it was said) brought the literary association, rather than the work itself with its famous lines:

Macbeth, Act IV, Scene I

The three witches, casting a spell
Round about the cauldron go;
In the poison'd entrails throw.
Toad, that under cold stone

Days and nights hast thirty one
Swelter'd venom sleeping got,
Boil thou first i' the charmed pot.

    Double, double toil and trouble;
    Fire burn and cauldron bubble.
Fillet of a fenny snake,
In the cauldron boil and bake;
Eye of newt, and toe of frog,
Wool of bat, and tongue of dog,
Adder's fork, and blind-worm's sting,
Lizard's leg, and howlet's wing,
For a charm of powerful trouble,
Like a hell-broth boil and bubble.

    Double, double toil and trouble;
    Fire burn and cauldron bubble.
Scale of dragon, tooth of wolf,
Witches' mummy, maw and gulf
Of the ravin'd salt-sea shark,
Root of hemlock digg'd i' the dark,
Liver of blaspheming Jew,
Gall of goat, and slips of yew
Sliver'd in the moon's eclipse,
Nose of Turk, and Tartar's lips,
Finger of birth-strangled babe
Ditch-deliver'd by a drab,
Make the gruel thick and slab:
Add thereto a tiger's chaudron,
For the ingredients of our cauldron.

    Double, double toil and trouble;
    Fire burn and cauldron bubble.

"Three Witches" is eerie with its literary nudge which certainly gives it an added dimension that opens the imagination to a literary landscape of what was in its time terrifying to some audiences. It underlines Kapoor's interest in scapegoating which is a regrettably fascinating aspect of our human culture and history.

The story of the three witches was included in Shakespeare's *Macbeth*. James I commissioned the play and thus it had to fulfill specific requirements, such as the inclusion of the character Banquo, who was supposed to be an ancestor of James I. It was to be performed for his court, probably in 1606. It is the shortest of all of Shakespeare's extant plays for this reason. Its length is closer to that of classical ancient Greek tragedy (plays) and has a more intense presentation throughout than his longer tragedies. James I of England and Scotland (formerly James VI of Scotland) was a fan so to speak of witch hunting and later popularized witch hunting in England where it was not nearly so prevalent and believed by less of the general public than it was in Scotland. After a witch trial there would usually be pamphlets circulated to justify the execution of the alleged witches and to inflame the public against them. After an initial interest in witches and witchcraft, James I quickly introduced new draconian laws against alleged witches that were very misogynistic. Eventually, James I seems to have lost some of his interest in the hobby. In the last nine years of his reign, only 5 witches were executed, compared with the very considerable number in the first years of his reign, including the North Berwick witch trials of 1590 in Scotland, in which James himself took part. It implicated over 70 people. Many of them confessed under severe torture and were executed.

He became the only monarch to have written a treatise on witchcraft when he published his *Daemonologie* 1597 (literally, the science of demons). In this work Kapoor is also taking on the history of scapegoating in the late renaissance era UK, and the scapegoating and scapegoated witches as well.

Kapoor's "Three Witches" are witches of our time rather than Shakespeare's as they do not invoke terror. Instead, they seem like sculptural forms that can tell a tale of a metaphorical relation to the fantasy of another time, that carries racist language by the very scapegoating and scapegoated witches in the play. Interestingly it is questionable whether actual witches in Europe even have existed in the first place.

Kapoor seemed to be interested in how to match what he wanted to express with what people actually experienced. He appeared to be completely willing to separate himself from his own views. He did disagree with us on points but seemed to be not arguing but trying to look for any possibility improve his work.

The next day I came back to look at his exhibit alone and I was surprised to find Kapoor was also there. He warmly came over and spent more time explaining his mild challenge to Da Vinci's artistic statement on art without order. He told me after my responses that I should be a writer rather than an artist.

The undercurrent of scapegoating is an on-tap possibility for us all and is potentially present in the most mundane of circumstances. We live with this daily from the playground to the grave. In thinking about Kapoor's work, the "Three Witches," it becomes clear that scapegoating is a part of the experience of his sculpture. Witches, or those presented as being witches, are given lines by Shakespeare, using scapegoating language, and fear of the other, which they themselves are. On the surface it appears to be one thing, but thinking about how the characters behave and what they say, it becomes something else.

In viewing his sculpture with its title and the import of that in mind, it opens to a larger picture of who we are as humans and how we behave in groups and our response to perceived others as apart from the group and other groups. Ultimately it is how we treat others that are seen as outside or different from, or not trying to be a part of a group or even a larger society. Scapegoating is a group's way of confirming a social hierarchy and maintaining control of the larger group or society, according to French anthropologist René Girard, and it is not very pleasant to look at closely. We are all involved in some way of thinking in scapegoating patterns, however subtle, and have been so since our first organized societies. According to Girard it is the very foundation of a society itself.

Racist graffiti amounting to scapegoating is, unintentionally, part of Kapoor's recent sculpture "Dirty Corner" (2011-15). It appears as a huge hollow steel almost pitcher plant turned on its side. It is about 60 metres long and 8 metres tall at its highest point. (As viewers enter, and start walking, they slowly become disoriented, losing their perception of space. It gets progressively darker before it becomes total darkness. This makes viewers use other senses to move in the space).

It was displayed in the gardens of Versailles where it received considerable media attention. It was eventually dubbed "the queen's vagina" by some in the French media, and offended some of the viewing public. Its temporary presence in the gardens of Versailles is a contrast that provokes thought, the imagination both prurient and not, and is a humorous metaphor surrounded by flowers and budding vegetation.

It is surprising that it was vandalized three times with racist graffiti, some of it anti-Jewish and reminiscent of what we would expect from the three witches.

Kapoor said in response:

> Dirty Corner *has become the vehicle for the expression of our anxiety of "the other" and emphasis that Art is a focus for our deepest longings and fears. It is urgent that we show our solidarity with the oppressed the downtrodden and those of our brothers and sisters in need.*
> *As the artist I have—for the second time—to ask myself what this act of violence means to my work. The sculpture will now carry the scars of this renewed attack. I will not allow this act of violence and intolerance to be erased.* Dirty Corner *will now be marked with hate and I will preserve these scars as a memory of this painful history. I am determined that Art will triumph.*
>
> (Anish Kapoor, 6 September 2015)

Yayoi Kusama

Thoughts on Infinity Mirrors

The visual rhythms of the polka dots resemble the patterns
in her infinity rooms which seem to me to be similar to the patterns
in some Japanese Buddhist temple art. This aesthetic feel or
tone is in much of her almost rhythmically comforting work.
Daniel Pouliot / Creative Commons, Kusama Pumpkin at Naoshima

Yayoi Kusama, in seeking to be an artist in the western sense, was at odds with the traditional Japanese approach to art when she was young and living in Japan. (The west being that of the extreme individual path, the east being predominantly more part of a group tradition with the idea of "the nail that sticks out must be hammered down"). It was her only option, going to the west. New York allowed her to transform to a western sense of self. That would have been very difficult for her, had she stayed in Japan.

Kusama's "infinity nets," as she originally called them, are from her own hallucinations, her earliest work using polka dot fields. She drew her first one at the age of 10. They seem to be perceptive abstracted variations of the predominantly Buddhist art of the culture that was around her. This artistic culture of patterns includes Buddhist temple art, which has similar comforting patterns or visual rhythms. This continues to influence her later work.

She started working in a military factory starting at age 13 in 1942 during the Second World War, sewing parachutes for the Japanese military. She remembers the times of darkness in the factory, the air raid sirens, and seeing American bombers flying overhead in broad daylight. Around this time she was sent by her mother to spy on her father's affairs. This greatly affected her view of sex. After the war, aged 19, she studied Nihonga traditional Japanese painting at a local arts and crafts college. She quickly tired of this. She continued to study art despite her family's strong disapproval. Through her persistence, she managed to move to the U.S. in the late 50s and was living in New York by 1958.

Kusama said about her painting *Flower (D.S.P.S)* 1954:

One day I was looking at the red flower patterns of the tablecloth on a table, and when I looked up I saw the same pattern covering the ceiling, the windows, and the walls, and finally all over the room, my body and the universe. I felt as if I had begun to self-obliterate, to revolve in the infinity of endless time and the absoluteness of space, and be reduced to nothingness. As I realised it was actually happening and not just in my imagination, I was frightened. I knew I had to run away lest I should be deprived of my life by the spell of the red flowers. I ran desperately up the stairs. The steps below me began to fall apart and I fell down the stairs spraining my ankle.

In some of her infinity rooms we are reminded of ourselves. It is easier to have less notice of ourselves in the mirror reflections on the walls in the darker, more blue themed rooms. There are many little lights that make us associate with stars in space. The inclusion of ourselves in the infinity room by our own reflections in the mirrors can make us feel part of this sense, or feel self-conscious at perceiving ourselves. There is a finite feeling of trying to overcompensate from being reminded of myself in this space. At one point it is the feeling of disembodied space or transcendental space that is presented. For me it was impinged on by my own image being included in that space. The self-conscious moment is an effect of her art, in that our own experience is attached to our self-conscious selves and separation from this is sometimes difficult.

Her aesthetic is elemental, which she calls "environmental" art. But it is the influence of Buddhist temple art and gardens that runs all through her work and her titles sometimes seem like they are extensions of Buddhist vision aesthetics. Titles such as *self-obliteration* (1967) *infinity room* (1965), *infinity nets*, and *Ascension of Polka dots* seem Buddhist in influence.

> A polka-dot has the form of the sun, which is a symbol of the energy of the whole world and our living life, and also the form of the moon, which is calm. Round, soft, colourful, senseless and unknowing. Polka-dots can't stay alone; like the communicative life of people, two or three polka-dots become movement ... Polka-dots are a way to infinity.
> —Yayoi Kusama, in *Manhattan Suicide Addict*

Also her fractal image box in the 2018 *Infinity Mirrors* exhibit that included a reflection of the viewer and the second alternate viewer in the second window may be seen to distract or include the self in being carried away by the space of eternity.

This is not always the case. She creates fractal-peep rooms in the shape of balls such as the one in her 2018 world travelling exhibit where we are not included in reflection in the work, and the space opens to a perceived strange fractal-planetary world. That is what appeals to this sense of imaginative engagement with selfless space and being. That is being included in everything as though we could even be viewing the world in the ancient Greek imaginative sense of our eyes reaching out from us and our projected vision is going out from our eyes and pulling these things in space into our perception rather than the optical sense of our eyes refracting light as is actually the case and how our time generally perceives it.

At the end of her exhibits there is often a room or section where the viewers are given small sheets of sticky polka dots and told they can put polka dots on all the walls and chairs. There is something so delightfully democratic about this, conveying obviously that you too are, and can be, part of this.

Marina Abramović

2009 New York

The Artist is Present. Performance artist Marina Abramović at the Museum of Modern Art in New York City, April 2010. Thousandrobots, Creative Commons.

*After 40 years of people thinking you're insane
and you should be put in mental hospital, you finally
actually get all these acknowledgments, it takes
such a long time to be taken seriously.*

—Marina Abramović, *The Artist is Present*

The main question since she started performance art has been: Why is this art? The medium of this art form is the human body.

Her art practice includes the possibility of violence, and in some cases violence itself.

Much of her work is engaging her audience in a group or co-experience of her art. Some of these performances are called interventions.

Perhaps her most well know and most committed performance is *Rhythm 0*, from 1974.

There were a number of objects on a table in front of her, and the people in the gallery could use the objects on or against her. The objects included a gun and a bullet on the table and it could be used on her without prosecution.

RHYTHM 0
Instructions
There are 72 objects on the table that one can use on me as desired.

Performance.
I am the object.
During this period I take full responsibility.
Duration 6 hours (8pm—2am)
1974
Studio Morra, Naples

"If someone wanted to put the bullet into the pistol and use it, I was ready for the consequences. I said to myself, *Okay, lets what happens.*

"For the first three hours, not much happened— the audience was being shy with me. I just stood there, staring into the distance, not looking at anything or anybody; now and then, someone would hand me the rose, or drape the shawl over my shoulders, or kiss me.

"Then, slowly at first and then quickly, things began to happen. It was very interesting: for the most part, the women in the gallery would tell the men what to do to me, rather than do it themselves (although later on, when someone stuck a pin in me, one woman wiped the tears from my eyes). For the most part, these were just normal members of the Italian art establishment and their wives. Ultimately, I think the reason I wasn't raped was that the wives were there."

—from Abramović, Marina. *Walk Through Walls: A Memoir.* 2016. Page 68-9

This kind of performance art is apt to bring out what is underneath the thin veneer of culture. Someone did put the loaded gun to her head and was pushing her finger to the trigger when a struggle broke out over control of the gun. The individual was expelled from the gallery but the audience went on behaving in a way they would never have been able to in normal society or circumstances. She was cut with an object and she bled considerably.

At 2 a.m., after the gallerist said that the performance was finished, Abramović approached the audience in the gallery. Most immediately left the gallery not wanting to meet, or be near the artist.

This performance is still frequently talked about to this day. She brought the primitive horrific side of humanity out. This shocked the audience, as they were, more than many of them initially realized, part of the art. Many perhaps unwittingly were unable to realize how close they too can come to violent and brutish behaviour, that we ourselves are also little more than the thinnest level of persona we identify with in ourselves. This is all of us; we are capable of things that are frightening.

The next day the gallery was inundated with phone calls of people from the night before apologizing for their behaviour.

March 9th to May 31st 2010, the artist was present in the MOMA (Museum of Modern Art) gallery in New York City every single day, all day, 6 days a week. It was a performance of endurance. She sat across a simple table in a large cleared square. There was nothing on the floor. She would then just look at the people as they would come one by one to sit across from her and look into her eyes. There was no verbal communication. During the last weeks, some people would line up all night to have the chance to sit across from her. In all, it is estimated, about 750,000 people lined up to see her, though only about 1,000 sat across from her. Abramović commented at how much pain there was in some sitters. Many people cried from their experience. There is an intensity to be looked at without any distraction, directly looked into, but not stared at. This experience was moving for some. Others saw it as a stunt; still others commented on her rock star-like status, and those lining up as her groupies. One middle-aged well spoken man had a tattoo on his arm with the number of times he had engaged with Marina Abramović.

This business of pain that Abramović engages with—her own, and that of the public's—is interesting for sure. Her art sometimes seems like an understanding of pain. If she had a gentler childhood, she would not be able to do what she does. If her much talked about bumpy childhood with her stern war hero parents had been truly abusive, she would perhaps been too damaged and never have been able to become an artist on this level. When I think of the many people who stood in line to see her (in *The Artist is Present*), and some of those who were so deeply effected by the experience, I think her background was perfect for being a performance artist. Those who come from extreme suffering very very rarely are able to reach for art. It is almost always others with less pain (yes, standard cliché here) that represent their pain in art. A grumpy art lover might add that this is mostly for the petty climbers and posers though there is a kind of voyeuristic circus about this.

Richard Hambleton

Shadow Man

Richard Hambleton, Shadow Man (C. 1979 Hank O'Neil)

Richard Hambleton was born in Vancouver in 1952 and earned an advanced diploma from the Vancouver school of art in 1975.

He almost immediately created public art murder scenes, and mass murder scenes, in 15 major cities across the United States and Canada, from the mid- through the late-1970s. In these, he created scenes that looked as if people were killed there. He would get volunteers to pose on the ground as murder victims while he would trace their outlines, so the result would appear like police chalk outlines of homicide victims. He would then splash red paint on parts of the outlines, giving the appearance of crime scenes. He received a considerable amount of unexpected press from this work. He was even suspected of being involved in such crimes.

His work was so visceral that some in the public thought there must be some truth to the staged homicide scenes. Some in the news media even questioned him on camera about these works, questioning if they were entirely fictional and just "art". He said: "I wanted to create realism—there are no boundaries, we are all vulnerable."

It was a kind of street art where we stumble onto it and are shocked.

"People began to think I was murdering people."

When he eventually made the news, he said: "This was part of the art. The media was part of it."

He later continued in New York with "I only have eyes for you." Of this time he says: "I figure painted all around the city. It was done on blueprint paper, so it would fade away in months." These figures caused people to go out looking for his street art. He had become an anonymous street artist with a following public.

In 1979 he started painting his famous *Shadow Man* works on walls around New York. At this time, Hambleton felt more connected to the night. His images were scary; they captured the lurking possibility of a dark side or potential violence. "If anything I am the shadow behind the figure." People would go around looking for his *Shadow Man* figures. Later Keith Haring and Basquiat were street artists in the same art circle as Hambleton and had similar followings.

Richard Hambleton, Shadow Man (C. 1979 Hank O'Neil)

Richard Hambleton, Shadow Man (C. 1980 Hank O'Neil)

In 1979 Hambleton took his street art to Europe while having shows of his paintings in European galleries. He painted his *Shadow Man* street paintings in public, all over many of the larger cities in western Europe.

Drugs and art went together in the New York art world of the 1980s. AIDS also contributed to the downfall of the New York art scene of that circle. He lost himself to drugs shortly after this. His fall was completed when he started making seascape paintings with his own blood when he ran out of money for paint. This became his new style of painting and the art scene was not interested in this work.

At the time he was admired in the New York art world even more than Haring and Basquiat.

His un-saleable seascape paintings destroyed his career. As a result he was degraded and mostly forgotten. One account said he was painting the cloud of blood in the syringe.

Art organizers Vladimir Roison and Andy Valmorbida brought Richard Hambleton back to the public along with a Giorgio Armani sponsored reshowing of his work called "Richard Hambleton—New York" in 2009.

His *Shadow Man* paintings and street art are instantly recognizable to a wide public. The haunting presence of these figures in the imagination even years after first seeing them proves the lasting power of this work, even if it grew out of a more extemporary approach and ephemeral expectation of the lifespan of his original shadow paintings. Banksy has even noted the influence of Richard Hambleton on his own street art.

Hambleton's *Shadow Man* paintings are painted so quickly. His seemingly unthinking skill is no doubt influenced by his street art, where he had to paint at considerable speed, in the field, so to speak. When he paints them on canvas it is a testament to his skill. He did not use stencils in his street art like Banksy does.

Hambleton was always creating, even at his lowest points, as when he had to move into an abandoned gas station for shelter. More so than many artists, he was a constant creator for himself when there was no other audience. To have turned his back on the art world when he was at the top of it is unbelievable for most, but shows he was not about the art scene that drove the art market of that time. He had what Tolstoy describes as utter sincerity in creation. Hambleton for all his struggles, was a true artist.

Banksy Show (unauthorized)

Toronto

Banksy opening

It is almost impossible to think of Banksy without considering the art and street art of Richard Hambleton who painted his iconic *Shadow Man* figures around New York City starting in the late 70s and then becoming iconic by the mid 80s. Banksy is indebted to this generation of street artists which later included Keith Haring and Jean Michel Basquiat.

This exhibit, an unauthorized retrospective of Banksy, is mostly of works made in his earlier period with a significant amount of work from about a decade ago. It does not include much of his well known recent work. Steve Lazarides says in the following interview that these shows are necessary because museums do not show Banksy's work.

The fact that exhibitions like this—with 35-dollar a ticket entry prices—exist means the public at large is interested in this work. It is also evidence that Banksy's reputation has taken on a life of its own.

It is a bit of a circus affair, this kind of exhibit, occupying a large warehouse space that sometimes holds Burning Man events in Toronto. The feel is that this kind of exhibition is more for the suburban set who want to get close to street art, and thereby have an edge of some kind, commensurate with something accepted as cool that they can now see up close. It is hard not to laugh at how the show was presented. Let's be honest, Banksy bar in large letters to partying suburban bourgeois people around it is hilarious stuff, the kind of thing that I don't generally associate with the public persona of Banksy.

It is notable that this is a for profit exhibit at a large private event space rather than an exhibit at an actual gallery. This seems to be far from the initial spirit of Banksy. Banksy, to his credit, claims to have no part in this show.

The fact that a print was stolen from this exhibit in Toronto on June 14th, 2018—just before the opening, made world news, and made the exhibit world known—was a kind of free advertising. The video footage of the theft is rather amateur in appearance. Both of the camera angles in the 46-second clip are listed as camera 01. A figure, probably a woman, in dark clothes, wearing a hat, and well covered around her/his face and neck, is seen entering the room. It is well lit but not bright. The figure walks in a sneaky way as if he/she were a character out of child's cartoon being thief-like. There should have been silly music to accompany this

on the publically released video, as it looks so ridicu-
lously fake that it is painful. It would be embarrassing
if Banksy were involved with such a lame stunt. I asked
a cop near the exhibit about this and he laughed, but
refused to comment.

Much of Banksy's work speaks for itself. It is popular art that engages the average person. It is a kind of democratic art that is very appealing to those who may not otherwise be interested in art or might feel that high brow art is not for them or people of their background.

The extroverted appeal of Banksy's work, and his/her appeal to the average person as being fully able to understand, and be directly engaged with his work, is a hallmark of Banksy's enduring appeal.

This is from a brief interview the day before the opening, with Steve Lazarides, Banksy's long time gallerist and photographer, who stopped working with Banksy in 2008.

Wild Style Cow

"When Banksy told me he had asked a farmer if he could paint his cows, I pointed out the farmer probably thought he was going to bring some watercolours and an easel... Not actually paint his cows"

Steve Lazarides

Ewan Whyte: You look like a mother bird, plagued by her progeny, and at this point you're sick of it (interviews).
(Laughter)
    There's a sort of mystical feel to Banksy's work.
Steve Lazarides: Yeah.
Whyte: I wonder if you could talk about that a little bit?
Lazarides: I think it's just because he's been that kind of, you know, person that no one can ever reach. That a

lot of the exhibitions he did only lasted for three days. So people have, people have seen the book, people see stuff on the website. But people have rarely seen stuff in the flesh. He does fewer and fewer pieces out on the street nowadays, and when they do it becomes of epic proportions and people travelling from across the globe to go and see it. I think he's just, I don't know, I think everybody, you know, in this kind of Kardashian age where everyone wants to be famous, it's that thing that with somebody who is famous, to not want to be known. It's a complete … like people cannot compute. I think it sets him apart from almost everyone else.

Whyte: There's a kind of dignity to that.

Lazarides: Yeah, for sure.

Whyte: I wouldn't want to know who he is.

On the mystical—you know the, the child here …

[About the youth kneeling in a gesture of prayer in front of a large section of street art framed as though it were stained glass. He has spray painting equipment immediately in front of him, so he must have just painted it].

The prayer, but the secular sense …

Lazarides: There's a lot of kind of whimsical kind of things in his artwork and I, it's like the girl in bloom that everyone thinks is such a lovely image. I find quite sad because I think it's a girl who's in the blue. There's a lot people saying that she's letting it go on purpose so it's kind of, you know, it's a, it's a hard one to kind of nail down, but it definitely comes through his work, and it definitely got the general public definitely taking it to heart. He's like a modern Robin Hood, I think, you know, people like to get behind. Not that he's an underdog but I think people like to get behind someone that they think's got, like, a strong moral compass.

Whyte: Yes.

Lazarides: And I think that's part of what adds to his kind of mystique.

Whyte: Can you comment personally on Banksy and mysticism—is he a mystical person, do you think?

Lazarides: Ah, *[hesitates]* I'm not going to comment, I'm not going to give anything away.

[He laughs]

Whyte: Fair enough. With this you, I think right away of Kenneth Clark, talking about clearstory, flying buttress, you get this, and no matter what you would put there, you have a mystic gesture. It's just whatever is in this space here it's going to be.

Lazarides: I wanted it as the final piece, because I think, you know, it's the piece that people would stand in front of for hours. And it's not … it's only been seen once, and that was in Los Angeles back in 2008. So it's been stuck in storage ever since just because it's such a big piece. Well, it's really nice to actually break it out.

Whyte: It's a really nice (work).

Lazarides: Someone complained earlier that they didn't think there was enough work in it, which I thought was quite odd.

Whyte: I think that the public has an expectation of large scale work? But there are …

[Referring to the piece where several people are standing on a wrecked, or burned out tireless car holding an American flag in a mock reference to the soldiers raising

the U. S. flag at Iwo Jima toward the end of a battle in the Second World War.]

Lazarides: There are ... it's like, you know, that's the biggest piece he ever made, he didn't make many pieces this size. And that's the second biggest piece he ever made.

[Laughter]

You know. It was rare that pieces ever got made at this size. Really, kind of ... and what we've done is put in the really important ... Myst ... Like you say, mystical, and mythical ... has that commentary with him kind of running with the police. You have, you know, two of the most iconic images he's ever done.

Plus the kind of the Keep it Real Monkey, you've got you know very early piece from back in Bristol in 2000. So I think he was trying to keep it so there was a good kind of cross section of work I think it's important from his career. And I don't think it's necessarily just about the big blockbuster piece which there are any. You know we went to the market to try and buy one of these for a client.

We went to 10 people, not a single person was selling it, not even for an astronomical amount of money. And then I think the print room for me is the most important room in the whole shop. This is really where it all started and I think this is where his popularity was really garnered. And the thing. I think I'm proudest of being involved in with him is making art accessible to the masses, kind of, you know.

These prints were like 35 quid each, they sold to Joe Public. It wasn't kind of art buyers that were buying it back then. And, you know, we've made a generation people that didn't think that they liked art, like art. And buy stuff to go in their homes. And I think this is a really important kind of step through his career.

Whyte: It's amazing moment when the average person suddenly feels part of something that was once exclusive.

Lazarides: Yeah, innit, but it was the other way round with him. It was, instead of a trickle down, it was a kick up. So it started with, you know, Joe Public and you can see it, like, forced its way up through the ranks. And even now, you know, the museums and stuff still don't take it seriously. Which is annoying.

Whyte: Really?

Lazarides: Yeah.

Whyte: Well, he's, he's not he's not in (any museums)?

Lazarides: The only reason we're doing shows like this is because museums don't.

Whyte: Ah, I'm surprised by that.

Lazarides: Then this time round we put stuff into this show that, you know, people want to see more, like the old pictures … pictures of him actually putting something up on the street.

There's more context this time than there ever was before. The biggest spread of works, this time, you know these, they're authenticated street pieces.

Whyte: So this is one of two street pieces in the show?

Lazarides: Yeah.

Whyte: And that's the other kind (of) one.

Lazarides: That's in Bristol.

Whyte: Nice.

Lazarides: I think the only thing that's going to have in here is a, is a corruptured oil painting, you know from this whole kind …

Whyte: Berenike the Greek goddess of victory, (or carrier of victory) shortened to Nike of Samothrace.

[Laughter]

Lazarides: Bought from a garden center for like 200 bucks.

Whyte: That's terrifying (the camera for a face and head), but very funny. Even this, goddess of Victory. A city named after her, you know, everywhere all through mythology, the Iliad … I guess that's the, I guess, the complaint …

Lazarides: Yeah well he had a real thing about CCTV cameras.

Whyte: To stop the IRA, they had cameras, apparently, (was) that was the official excuse?

Lazarides: They had them all over London. Why this is still the most camera-ed city in the world. They say you can't leave your house …

You leave your house, you're probably tracked from leaving the house to work. But we never really sussed is that a lot of them aren't switched off. So when we did something we thought it would definitely have been picked up by the security coming through central London, and it wasn't.

Whyte: What year was it?

Lazarides: That would have been … 2007, 2008? Where he did one of his phone box stunts. We had like a folded-up phone box, it was in an alleyway.

And they came, the police came to the gallery, we thought this is it, time's up. And um, and there was no evidence. I was just like someone must have just dumped it there; it has nothing to do with us.

Whyte: That's great.

[Laughter].

Lazarides: You know I'm quite happy with, with the spread of works, in a kind of, you know, it's a journey through Banksy's work.

Whyte: Thank you.

Lazarides: My pleasure. Thank you very much.

When leaving the exhibit, the exit is through a gift shop. This is pretty funny when you consider Banksy's famous satirical film is *Exit Through the Gift Shop*.

This was one of the most ridiculous things I have seen in any art related event. I asked several of the workers about it and they generally liked the Banksy logos on the bags and mugs. I thought of the ridiculous Che Guevara hats worn by so many of those who have no idea what he actually stood for. His complex life and excessively murderous interpretation of revolution is now sterilized for most of his hat wearing fans. Members of the public carrying things in Banksy art bags is inevitable, and Banksy's persona has a shifting collective life of its own. I am not so sure Banksy would be pleased.

Janet Cardiff
The Forty Part Motet

(A reworking of "Spem in Alium,"
by Thomas Tallis [C.1567-72])
2001, 40-channel audio installation
with speakers and stands

"The Forty Part Motet by Janet Cardiff"
by jepoirrier is licensed under CC BY-SA

Some unsuspecting gallery goers may be suddenly struck, from a different part of a museum or gallery, with the sound of renaissance composer Thomas Tallis's 40-part motet[2] before they even reach the room where it is being exhibited. For most, it would likely be entirely unexpected to hear one of the most famous and profound pieces of high renaissance music in a contemporary art space. Putting such a piece of music in a such a space would be unusual. This is now a piece of contemporary art.

Upon entering the gallery or room, the viewer sees 40 black speakers, one for each singer in the original piece, arranged in a large loose circle or oval, supported on portable metal speaker posts and lifted to the head level of the average human height, in eight groups of five speakers, for the eight choirs or grouping of singers (soprano, alto, tenor, baritone, bass) that originally performed the work. Each speaker plays a separately recorded voice. All the separately recorded voices together are similar to a live performance. The music is a little over 10 minutes long with several minutes of the singers mutedly chatting to each other afterwards, before the piece automatically repeats.

---

2. **The text in Latin**

The text in English

Spem in alium nunquam habui	I have never put my hope in any other
Praeter in te, Deus Israel	but in Thee, God of Israel
Qui irasceris et propitius eris	who canst show both wrath and graciousness,
et omnia peccata hominum	and who absolves all the sins
in tribulatione dimittis	of man in suffering
Domine Deus	Lord God,
Creator caeli et terrae	Creator of Heaven and Earth
respice humilitatem nostrum	Regard our humility

This recording was made with members of the Salisbury Cathedral choir during the 2001 Salisbury Festival. A child soprano was used rather than a countertenor as would likely have been used during the Renaissance.

There are often benches in the middle area when this piece is exhibited, although in the National Gallery of Canada it was exhibited in the former older deconsecrated church area of the gallery that was included in the basement when the new building was built over it. This installation work has travelled around for exhibit to many galleries around the world and has proven to be a crowd pleaser regardless of where it is shown.

This work, *Spem in Alium* is not just any work of Renaissance music. It is unusual in its inspiration and its emotive power of sacred space. It is nearly 500 years old, and was written for an audience that would be very different from the listeners today. The fact that such antique art can still move considerable numbers of the public who are exposed to it is a testament to the work itself. But this kind of work is built on a long tradition of composition and a tradition of very educated and skilled musicianship in singers in order to perform the work itself. Most importantly there was an audience that was willing to receive such works and people willing to pay for them to be composed and performed.

When a listener hears this work, they are experiencing the tradition of music that goes back to the very beginning of the medieval era. It could only be on such traditions that art like this can be created.

Why chose this piece and not a work by say Palestrina, J.S. Bach's favourite composer who wrote music that continues to inspire and delight to this day? This piece is the perfect length of what the average person can intensely concentrate. Other works are much longer, but very few are anything close to this grand.

Why was such a work as *Spem in Alium* composed?

The work was written between 1567 and 1572 because of a specific event. A Florentine composer named Alisandro Striggio travelled to England in 1567 with his masterpiece, *Ecce beatum lucem*, a 40-part motet (*Behold the Blessed Light*). Its performance was greatly admired by London audiences at the time. There was a concern in England that there was no English composer who had any comparable piece of music. Presumably it was the Duke of Norfolk who commissioned Thomas Tallis to compose his 40-part motet as a response. It was a considerable undertaking even to attempt. Its success is a gift for our time in Janet Cardiff's presentation of this work. Kenneth Clark once quipped, when speaking of Raphael and plagiarism, that all great artists are borrowers, and he smiled.

The repeated overwhelming response of audiences to this work, *The 40 Part Motet*, is a reflection of how our time has an attraction to sacred art. Our time tends to consciously reject aesthetic art, as it does not usually satisfy our current political agendas. There is a dearth of it in contemporary galleries, and it is generally seen as off putting to many hip viewers of art. This work is about timelessness. And Janet Cardiff's presentation of it to the viewer is incredibly successful.

Yonghi Yang

Dear Pyongyang

Never has there been so much lying as in our day. Never has lying been so shameless, so systematic, so unceasing … Modern man—genus totalitarian— bathes in the lie, breathes the lie, is in thrall to the lie every moment of his existence.
—Alexandre Koyré, 1943[3] [p.143]

---

3. A. Koyré. "The political function of the modern lie." 143.

Zainichi-Korean director Yonghi Yang's *Dear Pyong-yang* (2006) provides a rare, moving window into the strange and terrible world of a totalitarian regime that has somehow managed to outlive its time in history. Her regard on this living relic of the 20th century horrors is all the more important as authoritarianism rises once again across the globe in our new century. Yang's intimate yet devastating window into life suspended on the diktats of North Korea's 'Dear Leaders' gives the viewer more than just a rare filmic glimpse into the brutality of this regime. It also recounts the tragic but exemplary story of Yonghi Yang and her family; one of exile and alienation, where family, love and even life are sacrificed on the pyre of a patriarch's ego and his unconditional devotion to a North Korean regime based entirely on lies.

Born in Japan to Korean parents who came to Japan in the early '50s in the aftermath of the Korean war, Yang and her three older brothers grew up in the Koreatown area of Osaka. As former colonial subjects, Koreans in Japan had endured an early 20th century history of anti-Korean sentiment, and exclusion. In the post-colonial period after WWII, their subaltern status took the form of relative impoverishment, some loss of civil rights, and insecurity. Her parents thus faced considerable hardship, and both invested in Korean associative life that provided a link to North Korea and kept alive the hopes of a return to a unified homeland. When she was five in 1971, her three brothers, only teenagers at the time, were repatriated to North Korea at her father's insistence, a country they had never lived in before. She did not see them again for eleven years.

It's hard to fathom what would bring a parent to make such a decision, and throughout her film, we see her trying to reach for an understanding after a childhood built on propaganda and lies, on missing brothers, on things impossible to speak of. Despite being born in Jeju, in the southernmost region of South Korea, Yang's father was ideologically and personally totally invested in the communist project of the North. She establishes at the outset his unconditional, rigid allegiance, how determined he was to send them all of his sons. Before the credits, the opening scene in her parents' cramped kitchen sets up the family dynamics. Yang gives her father 'New Year's money' and he counts out the yen to the running commentary and laughter of her mother. They celebrate her hard work and success, with her father commenting it was about time she brought a boyfriend home. She asks him what kind of boyfriend, and he smiles and answers, "anyone you love." His daughter, laughing and noting the film has it all on record, asks him if he really means "anyone". He qualifies: "No Americans, no Japanese," and goes on to reject Korean-Americans, or anybody who isn't "my kind of Korean."

The intimacy of the women's nervous laughter, their deference to him in small gestures of service, the playful tones used for vital questions, all introduce the structure of authority and her fear of being repudiated by her father should she refuse to marry according to his wishes or maintain her own allegiance to the regime. If she changed her nationality to South Korean, "He said it would mean a rejection of his life." The film draws the viewer in through the many unscripted, intimate interactions with her parents such as this, a focus that gives her film its emotional depth and critical force. She uses her camera to stage a mirror-game, where the big lies of state and the quotidian lies of the fanaticized patriarch constantly reflect one another, in a sort of *mise-en-abyme*. We see real affection in these family scenes, in many there are teasing, laughter, warm exchanges. In one striking scene, the father sits in his underwear, and sings a Korean poem:

> [S]weet briers bloom and fall
> in our island village
> A schoolteacher comes to the
> village with migrating birds
> An 18 year old falls in love
> With the teacher, a single man.
> My love, don't go back to Seoul
> Please don't go

Yet at times it's excruciating to watch him as he responds to her questions, apparently oblivious to the pain we read between her lines.

Yang's parents joined the some 600,000 Koreans who stayed in Japan following the end of WWII and the Korean war, although the great majority (1.4 million) had decided to return. Life in the '50s and '60s was very difficult for *chōsenjin* (Korean), a term that designated their foreignness as well as their inferior status. Though most Koreans in Japan were from the South, many identified more closely with the North, reflected in the greater popularity among Koreans of the communist project and the particular brand of nationalism that was animating it. In 1955, Koreans who had been active in a pro-North organization re-founded it under a new name, The General Association of Korean Residents in Japan (known in Korean by the shorthand *Chongryun*.) The group created a youth and women's league, writers', artists' and scientists' associations, athletic associations and merchant and entrepreneurs' groups.

Most importantly, the organization also opened more than 160 pro-North Korean schools which gave instruction in Korean.[4] Yang says of her schooling, "In those days, the ideological content of Kim Il Sung was incorporated into the curriculum of the schools." Her mother was also heavily involved in the organization, and her parents forbade any criticism of the fatherland.

---

4. S. Ryang. "The Rise and Fall of Chongryun—From Chōsenjin to Zainichi and beyond." The Asia-Pacific Journal. 14(11): 5.

Their childhood was one of indoctrination in North Korean propaganda, while enjoying the freedoms of life in Japan. Yang and her brothers secretly listened to the forbidden music of the Beatles yet grew up in a culture that treated them as relative outsiders.

Chongryun soon commanded mass support among Koreans in Japan. The organization had local headquarters running many smaller groups in every Japanese prefecture. While ostensibly committed to the North Korean Marxist programme, the movement was largely fuelled by nationalist fervour. The group was tolerated as they explicitly avoided involvement in Japanese politics and didn't request civil status or rights.[5] Yang's father, fanatically devoted to the cause, was one of the early leaders in *Chongryun*. The family thus held some respect in Osaka's Koreatown. Yang's father explains to the camera that "after the successful Soviet revolution many people thought that revolutions could succeed in their own countries," referring to the hopes among a great majority of Koreans in Japan that they too might one day join the reunited fatherland, one that had thrown off the colonial yoke and was building a radically new society of equality, opportunity and prosperity.

The stateless situation of *Chongryun* Koreans in the 1960s and '70s created the ideal conditions for spreading North Korean propaganda about the glorious new nation that was being built; stable jobs, high quality education, and good housing seemed like an excellent

---

5. Ibid. 6.

alternative to their difficult life in Japan. Thus in 1971,
Yang's brothers, the youngest only fourteen, were sent to
live in a country they had never been to and from which
they knew they would not return. Yang shows archival
footage of the massive repatriation event of 1971, where
her brothers joined thousands of other Koreans on the
repatriation ship Man Gyeong Bong for its maiden
voyage from Niigata Port in Japan to Wonsan, North
Korea on August 20. In 1972, the ship carried a massive
inventory of lavish gifts from the *Chongryun* to Kim Il
Sung for his sixtieth birthday. The zeal for repatriation
only began to die down in the late 1980s, largely because many had begun to see for themselves the realities
of life in the revolutionary fatherland. Over time, the
inferiority associated with the term *chōsenjin* gave way
to a new status for Korean-Japanese, and by the 1990s
the term *zainichi,* which became associated with cool
Korean pop culture.[6]

Beginning in 1981, Koreans were finally able to
obtain permanent residency in Japan, which meant
they could have re-entry permits, although often with
difficulty and some humiliation. Despite the lack of
diplomatic relations between North Korea and Japan,
Chongryun Koreans were allowed to visit their families
in the North on humanitarian grounds.[7] The ferry between Niigata and Wonsan became a route for family
reunions, and we see Yang and her parents board it,

---

6. Ibid. 10-11.
7. Ibid. 8.

more than two decades after they were first permitted, 30 years after her brothers left, under the weight of massive suitcases full of clothing and other goods. No doubt her father's position made it possible for them to make these regular, albeit brief visits, and for Yang to film in this extremely closed and media-hostile country. To be allowed to film in North Korea is a remarkable attestation to someone's loyalty.

It is never explained why Yang's father sent the boys there alone, rather than take the entire family. Perhaps he had important work to do for the *Chongryun*, but perhaps it is more honest to see the sacrifice of his sons to the fatherland as a means of obtaining not so much a better life for them in North Korea, as cementing his own importance as a diasporic leader. For while we can understand how Koreans were taken in by the onslaught of North Korean propaganda in the early decades, especially given the very real hardships of life in Japan as *chōsenjin*, it is considerably more difficult to explain why men like Yang's father continued to serve the North Korean cause with the same blind devotion even after they were finally able to visit. Many who visited were disgusted by the false picture presented by *Chongryun* propaganda; appalled by the terrible conditions, worried about their relatives' safety, they grew disenchanted with the organization. It was simply impossible to deny the reality of crushing material hardship, constant surveillance and fear of denunciation. Yang recounts how her mother tore up the first pictures the boys sent her from North Korea before her father could see them, because they had become so thin.

It's often hard to watch the submissive devotion of the good Confucian wife protecting her husband from the consequences of his authoritarian decisions. It's hard to understand her own continued devotion to the Great Leader, given what he did to her children. It becomes clearer as the film progresses that the sacrifice of sons enabled the father to create a social life in Japan where he could enjoy status and the admiration of his peers, free of state surveillance or denunciation by neighbours. Though were there to be denunciations, his wife and children have solid grounds. Perversely, as she shows so powerfully, this possibly naïve, but also profoundly selfish decision, nonetheless leads to the gradual destruction of this family over the years, like a long, slow starvation.

Children line up in front of a mural in Pyongyang, North Korea

Before the trip, there are numerous scenes of the family packing up boxes of goods to send to the brothers. While her mother is constantly sending boxes to her family in North Korea, she still often says: "Our family lives well because they are taken care of by our great leader." She advises her sons: "Make an effort to live like locals even if it is difficult." In these scenes, we can see the existential necessity of the lie for the father, through the careful protection of his wife and Yang's inability to form the words of accusation we realize she surely harbours. She moves around him on soft cat feet, teasing him, jollying him along; we can tell that she's not simply afraid that her father will reject her, she seems to be aware that these lies are the very glue holding her family together.

The voyage is oddly calm, the seas flat, the interior of the vessel decorated with posters serving as North Korean propaganda. There's a musical performance by three salmon satin-clad women in the stateroom. She films her parents giggling in their small bunk-bed cabin. One of her most poignant lines of the film, wistful and understated, comes as she gazes out on the ocean-scapes during the crossing: "My brothers left here thirty years ago. I wondered how they lived and what they could be thinking about." This fatherland was strange, and she could not really understand it, nor fathom her parents' devotion. Her voice speaks over an old black-and-white photo of her brothers before they depart, introducing us to them through a baby sibling's eye: "Kona, who was easy-going, should be ok, since he could make friends anywhere." She pans to the youngest: "Konmin, who was 14 then, was flexible enough to be able to adapt anywhere." Now the eldest, Kono, whose handsome profile she lingers on: "Kono couldn't live without coffee and classical music when he was in Japan. He listened to Beethoven on his headphones all day long. I was barely five when he spoke to me passionately about music."

She goes on to explain that when they arrived in North Korea, all Western music was banned; but, "times have changed, and now only Western classical music is per-mitted. So I sent many CDs of Chopin and Rachmaninoff to Kono." During the voyage, Yang also gives us foot-age from earlier visits to Kono's tiny apartment, where we meet his son Ursin, who is feted for finally entering the Pyongyang Music and Dance College's Elementary School. His Auntie's CDs have been put to good use, and we see him perform in a cramped, narrow room of their flat. The patriarch sits, grinning, as his little granddaughter who can't be older than 3, bounces around in her new Hello Kitty gear shrieking in delight, and thanks him with bows to general laughter. She's joined by her two cousins in turn: "Thank you for so many boxes, grandfather!"

Arriving in the North Korean port, her camera pans to massive signs atop the three tallest buildings which read, in ominous greeting:

"LIGHTNING ASSAULT"
"BLITZKRIEG"
"CRUSH ALL ENEMIES"

In Pyongyang, her covert footage is astounding. She films her parents bowing to the enormous bronze statue of Kim Jong Il. As they walk away, she teases them for stopping and behaving stiffly, as if her camera were a still-shot. Voice-off, she points out the massive, never-completed triangular building pointing skyward behind the Great Leader and remarks on its abandonment, a metaphor for the regime's lies and broken promises. She cannot share her parents' pleasure or reverence. Indeed, their obvious pleasure and pride is impossible to square with the realities of their sons' lives. We are shown a range of domestic scenes from Kona's tiny apartment, all filmed in her unscripted, almost amateur style. Now a young teen, Ursin performs a difficult piece by Liszt on a Yamaha piano; we imagine the Japanese family must have helped them obtain this rare luxury. His playing is good, and we realize that his parents have placed desperate hopes that his musical talent will offer him opportunities. The boy practices relentlessly, often in the dark.

Yang achieves a remarkable balance in these domestic scenes between the spontaneous laughter, warmth and teasing, and the awkward silences, the forced gaiety of her mother's chiding, her brother's heavy gaze, and always, the focus on the patriarch. With her camera's artless precision and a poignant piano score, she conveys a sense of silent desperation as they all perform for him the fiction of the nation's glory, of life improving, of his children's and grandchildren's chances.

Yang, who has been forced to swear her devotion to the fatherland her whole life and participate in this absurd, mortifying fiction, appears to be ready to, if not confront her father, at least try to explain to him that she is no longer devoted, and unwilling to swear to it. Her father is to attend a state ceremony, and we see them in their hotel room, her mother fussing over how to place a dozen or so large, heavy gold-coloured medals on his blazer.

Her parents in the next room, Yang stirs the pile of medals, picking them up, tossing them back almost carelessly, a gesture that belies her soft-spoken, gentle teasing. Voice off, she tells us of her incapacity to share in their excitement and pride; a scene moving and powerful in its emotional economy. The pomp and circumstance of the event, the enormous pride her father takes in being recognized are evidence of the primacy of the lie in this totalitarian world, and how elite status demands a commitment from which there can be no return. As Alexandre Koyré's reflections on totalitarianism of the '40s remind us: "Admission to the group takes the form of an irrevocable initiation; solidarity is transmuted into a passionate, exclusive bond; the symbols take on a sanctified meaning; fidelity to the group becomes the highest duty, nay, even the sole duty, of the members."[8]

In her own reflections on the modern lie and the logic of totalitarian regimes, Hannah Arendt underscores not only the power of the lie to overcome a world of facts, but the ways in which it destroys the space of politics as such, and, not content with isolating men from one another in the public realm, destroys at the same time that space of intimacy, affect and solace which is private life. Totalitarian regimes base themselves on loneliness, on the experience of not belonging to the world at all, and in this regard, they are uncannily like modern religious cults. I know this because I was raised in one.

Her father maintains his passionate commitment to the regime until the end of the film, even as he concedes: "I never thought the whole situation would turn out like this." As he restates his commitment one last time he also makes a huge concession to her, in accepting that she cannot share his allegiance, and promising that he will accept her even if she takes South Korean nationality. Her camera testifies to this in clear, honest, deeply empathetic way; her reticence only renders the film more poignant and heart-breaking. Yonghi Yang has accomplished a singular feat: not only does she bring us rare

---

8. Koyré, op.cit. 147.

footage of life in this notoriously closed and vengeful society, she reveals its human costs and horrors without ever saying a word against the regime, the Great Leader, or the patriarch who ruled her family. Yet her film will stand as a damning testimony to the bonfire of a single man's enormous personal vanity, and the threat that rising authoritarianism poses today to us all.

Works Cited

Koyré, Alexandre. 1945. "On the political implications of the modern lie."

Ryang, Sonia. 2016. "The Rise and Fall of Chongryun—From Chōsenjin to Zainichi and beyond." *The Asia-Pacific Journal*. 14(11): 1-16.

Yang, Yonghi. *Dear Pyongyang*. Directed by Yonghi Yang. 2005. Osaka Japan: 1h47min. Tidepoint Pictures/Typecast Releasing, 2006, DVD.

Alex Colville

From an interview with Alex Colville in 1967: "I am always concerned in a painting or in print with making a thing that seems absolutely authentic not generalized, and I suppose (it) is a reflection that whatever is here is now is important."

This was the painting voice of Alex Colville since he found his more individual style in the early 50s. He seemed to have never consciously moved from it for the rest of his creative life. There are instances of coincidence, or visual accidents that are inconsistent with this from time to time in his work, but on the whole he tried to consciously keep this project in the forefront of his art. As he gradually moved away from his nationally admired but not excessively original war paintings where he was an official war artist in the Canadian military during the Second World War, he struggled to find his own artistic voice. He slowly developed his contemporary approach involving a use of geometry and ordered design in the structuring of his paintings by a kind of intuitive accident.

"I did my first good painting in 1950, called *Nude and Dummy*."

It was at this point, he realized, he was able to make good paintings. He was 30. He was building a house shortly before he painted this work, and he had noticed that, in working on the architectural drawings, his process became one of organizing and measuring a space. He came to the point of viewing painting as being architectural. He used this method afterwards. This break from an intuitive approach to space in painting gave his work a depth he had never achieved before.

He later said: "It's only if you think you are some mad message bearer that you think geometry is beneath (you)."

Colville quoted Joseph Conrad in the film *The Splendor of Order*: "There's a wonderful phrase that Joseph Conrad used I've read, somewhere: 'I try to do the highest possible justice to reality, and I suppose this is basically what all artists are trying to do.'"

"One sees in nature, order," Colville said. "You look at a bug, for instance, you know it's quite amazing. Say an ant, the structure of the thing. Or you look at the branches on a tree, the kind of branching out thing and all this. Of course the Greek temples were an attempt and an extraordinarily successful one to capture in a man-made object the order they felt was innate in nature. That sense of order in immensely important to me."

His use of geometry is influenced by Renaissance painters. In many of his paintings by the mid-sixties there are often points of tension where our eye is brought to a focal point by his geometrical designs, and it would not matter what was there at the focal point, our eye is drawn to, it would carry a sense of imminence or menacing aspect, as in *Dog and Bridge*. It is his intuition that decides what is there but the rest is order.

His painting *Pacific,* 1967, of a man standing in front of a window and looking out onto the sea, his back to us and a target pistol on the table behind him, is an example of this. It is an interesting title, as pacific in Latin is quiet, calm, gentle, or mild. This painting is anything but that. But the water, fresh or salt, ocean or not, could be anywhere, so it is a title that also makes us think.

His work was not immediately appreciated and was frequently rejected when he sent in to exhibitions through the 60s. After representing Canada in the Venice Biennale in 1966, he started to gain international recognition.

His European art dealer Wolfgang Fischer, whom he met in 1966 during the Venice Biennale, expressed that there seemed to him a sense of angst in the paintings that was something German art collectors rather than the English speaking ones initially identified with.

What impressed me so much about Alex Colville, beyond his art, was his generosity. He was giving a lecture at the art school I was attending, and he noticed some of us young students standing in the hallway who did not have tickets to hear his lecture. We stood there in the hallway and listened. At the break he mentioned that we as young students should have been allowed inside, instead of selling tickets to the general public first. It may have been because I was the only student who lasted to the end of his long lecture still standing in the hallway, that he spoke with me for over an hour (in the first of several conversations with him over the next few years) about his art despite being pestered by staff at the art school. I asked him (what I would ask almost every prominent artist I met at the time) what he thought of Da Vinci's famous phrase "those who practice art without order are as those who willingly get on a ship without a rudder and set sail." He laughed. His response was very memorable about how order is something that can make art truly art. He acknowledged that there were many other artists working in freer forms or pop art and abstraction, but questioned if much of this work would last.

I asked Colville if putting in an element beyond the ordinary might add something else to his work in the same way geometry opened a new dimension to his work. I commented on the hound in field painting and how the background invokes associations in the forest beyond the field. I used the example of the painting of the *Dog and Priest* sitting where the man's face is obscured and his head appears in a way that makes the viewer possibly associate the man to the Egyptian god Anubis. He paused before he said he regretted that accident in his painting. He clearly seemed to have had heard it before.

His painting *Cyclist and Crow* (1981) is an example of his insistence of painting in the name brands of objects. The name Peugeot is on the bike prominently where the painting as a whole does not need it, for me, points away from the mundane. The here and now of a name brand in this particular composition, for me, points away from the mystical quality of the rest of the painting with the cyclist riding along the road with a sole crow flying low over a field with a far distant horizon line, with a thick forest above and behind it, blotting out any view of sky whatsoever. For me this painting would be stronger without the associative distraction of a name brand, but Colville thought differently.

Perhaps he is strongest where he has a larger mythical relation, that is in spite of himself. Colville resists this consciously and it is where it leaks into his paintings for me, he is at his best. He comments on how he is uneasy with this and I think it is interesting that he resisted it so much intellectually for when it is allowed to enter his art, Colville is for me, at his absolute best. *Dog and Priest* may be more than he intended, perhaps Colville's unconscious won out that day. We all know artists sometimes think they know what they mean by a work, but that is not always what they mean.

Victor Ekpuk

An Interview

Victor Ekpuk, *Blue Notes*

Ewan Whyte: What are Nsibidi symbols?

Victor Ekpuk: These are very old forms of communication that were active in precolonial Nigeria, among the peoples of southeastern Nigeria and southwest Cameroon also described by anthropologists as the Cross River region. This system of communication uses graphic symbols, pantomime, speech and placement of objects to communicate ideas. It was common amongst several mainly male secret fraternities. The pantomime aspect of the communication is performed as a choreography for public entertainment by members of these societies. Or, it could be coded communications among initiates. That is, they give each other sign languages through gestures, and the ability to decode or have more knowledge of the signs, ensures ones rise in the hierarchy of that knowledge system. I grew up within that culture, I'm Ibibio. My maternal grandfather Obong "Nwot nda" Asuquo Akpan, was a titled member of several male fraternities in his community, and was very knowledgeable, and engaged in the different aspects of these fraternities, like the Ekpe (Leopard) society, Ekpo and other elite societies of his time. I've seen Nsibidi up close either performative, inscribed or spoken.

I got interested in using it as a form of artistic notation while in college. I attended to the University of Ife, Obafemi Awolowo University. [Ile-Ife, heart of the Old Oyo Empire, it is the Yoruba ancestral-cultural home in the southwest of Nigeria, it also has a famous school of art] and it was there that I was introduced to the idea that my own African aesthetics were a very relevant form of self-expression as an artist. So rather than looking to the west for artistic inspirations, I was taught to look back, to look inwards.

Ewan: Please expand on the context of looking inwards.

Victor: So we were … my professors then were students of the negritude movement, a post independent ideology of black consciousness which swept most of Africa in the 1950. This idea of looking inwards, to our own ancestral aesthetics, for our own expression, be it in the visual arts, literature, architecture was a natural offshoot of that movement.

At the University of Ife art school was where I started to pay attention to the local visual culture in my immediate environment, the indigenous Yoruba motifs and expressions being one of them. I also came across works of other artists who have used, you know, other forms of traditional aesthetics in their works. I was really drawn to the works of Obiora Adechukwu, that was the first time, I saw Nsibidi used by an artist. And it occurred to me, well actually, I'm from this area of Nsibidi tradition, and I was familiar with it, so I started to look more closely. When I got back home on holidays, I went to older family members asking questions, the research sort of opened up a family history that I had not thought of, it revealed or brought back memories of my maternal grandfather and my maternal uncle as artists in their own right who active practitioners of the Ibibio culture. I recollected that my first encounter with Nsibidi was my time with my grandfather in his village where he was a well-known herbal healer, a titled man with high ranks in various male fraternities that utilize Nsibidi as a code of sacred communication.

For my purpose as an art student, I was drawn to graphic aspects of Nsibidi which I incorporated in my work.

Victor Ekpuk, The Face

Ewan: Are you using the language differently, Is it a different script from a normal spoken language?

Victor: Nsibidi not so much a spoken … Well. Well, let's talk about spoken language. Nsibidi could also be spoken language, but language spoken in ways that uses symbols in speech, rather than … not sure how to explain it. It is more like speaking in codes with meta-meanings where you think you understand but you don't, because it is not meant to be understood literally, and only members of the group learn the codes and understand its deeper meanings.

In terms of the "script," the graphic part of Nsibidi is not an alphabet at all, these are signs that connote ideas, and these ideas could be different based on the context in which it's used. So you're not going to find

... they are not symbols that represent sounds like the Roman alphabet.

Ewan: Is it similar in a way, say, to Egyptian hieroglyphs?

Victor: Yes, you could say that, but Egyptian forms are not as abstract as Nsibidi. Because in Nsibidi ideas are reduced to symbols in very abstract forms. Nsibidi seeks out and expresses the essence of form. Whereas in hieroglyphics you see full forms. And you can read through the pictographs, basically, you know, it's literal.

My approach to abstraction in my work by essentializing form is guided by the esoteric philosophy of Nsibidi. Through these long years of practice, I've come to internalize it in such that it's not so much that I'm writing Nsibidi per se, I have formed my own unique vocabulary so to speak. Some scholars argue that, well, maybe it's another form of Nsibidi, because it takes that same idea, that same aesthetic philosophy. I would say that Nsibidi is the foundation which I form my own new ideas about abstraction.

Victor Ekpuk, Shrine to knowledge

Ewan: You've created your own variation of the language.
Victor: Yes, my own variation of the language, so to speak, in the way, in how I now apply my own … if I wanted to draw, say, a human form, for instance, I would particularly look for the essence of that form, and then apply it in that way, and then I add other elements to it. My marks sort of tease the idea of writing, it is in that liminal space between writing and, well, art, so to speak. You know, and so on. I don't even try to analyze it too much. I just go, I just go with the flow. I let you, I let the viewer decide what they see., and how they feel about it. I'm much more interested in what I feel than trying to theorize about it.

Ewan: So, it's like metonymic language where something is said, but then there's something else where the symbol is metaphor. So it's a way of maximising your poetic expression.

Victor: Yes! And a symbol could be … once you leave it as it is without explanation, people will come to it from their own perspective of what they see, of how they experience that symbol. So. I'd like to leave my work at that, in that sense. But it doesn't mean that I don't express specific things. I prefer to leave it loose, and like you said, you know, you come into a space and you experience my work like a visual sensory poetry, and you can read what you feel out of it.

Ewan: That is powerful. The monumental scale of some of this, like the one that you did in the North Carolina Museum of Art?

Victor: I just I love to draw. And the ability to work at that scale, really, is always immensely satisfying. What I enjoy about drawing in that scale is walking into the piece and being engulfed by it. The North Carolina Museum of Art commissioned the piece as part of a maiden exhibition to open the new expanded African art galleries. It was nice to show alongside El Anatsui, Yinka Shonibare and Maryline Odundo all of whose works I admire.

That work was part of a series ephemeral drawing which probe an existential questions. I started a few years back a series of drawing I call "Drawing Memory" or "Meditation on Memory". I see memory as an ephemeral condition, which changes, shifts and is affected by circumstances. It could eventually get erased. I see memory as that which gives us our sense of identities, identities themselves are not eternally fixed conditions, it is always shifting and changing sometimes forced by circumstances. And to exemplify this, I mainly use non-permanent materials like chalk to draw this piece. The project always has a lifespan after which it must be erased for the work to be complete. It doesn't matter who erases it, or how it is erased, I always insist that the work be erased, for that work to be complete. For these projects I ask the institution I'm working with to document the process of making of the marking and the process of the erasure.

And the way that I see that is that we come into this world, we struggle, you know, to make money or whatever we do to survive in this physical universe, eventually, at some point(s), we have to leave the space, and something else will occupy that space. But no matter that our memory has been affected or erased, we are not always completely gone, sometimes the rudiments of our presence remain, traces of our individual or collective continues to exist, I would like to call this genetic memory.

After the erasure of the drawing, if you get close enough to the wall, you see the faint rudiments of the marks on the wall.. Through the years, I have taken a keen interest in the deep relationship/similarity of cultures of Africans in diaspora on the American continents and Africa continent, especially sub-Saharan Africa where millions of people were shipped out to be enslaved in the Americas. What I find at the core of these cultures is an unbroken persistence cultural or genetic memory that is beyond skin color. While there were attempts at erasure, the rudiments remain just below the surface. These observations were the impetus of "Meditation on Memory" series. My piece at the 12th Havana biennale was one of the most moving of the series for me, it was an homage to my ancestors who were taken from Ibibio, Efik and Ejagham lands in Nigeria and brought to Cuba and enslaved to work the sugar plantations. They retained their memory of origin in the Abakua society where traces of their African language, songs, dance and place of original homes are kept in secret. I created the entire work while listening to recorded Abakua chants. On the day of the opening of biennale, I invited members of the society to sing and perform within my installation space while I complete the piece. The connection and reunion was emotional and magical.

The piece at North Carolina Museum is one of those. I didn't approach the work with a preconceived notion of what I was going to do. Because usually when I do these projects, I want what is happening right there, and the history of that surrounding to inspire the piece.

In that space, I was surrounded by other art objects, both classical African objects and contemporarily pieces.

As I sat there and, you know, taking in the ambience of the space, "Opon Ifa" the Yoruba divinity board, spoke to me. The symbolism of the object was speaking loudly to me, both by the aesthetic form and the content. "Opon Ifa" is a divination board that Babalawo the priest of Ifa in Yoruba religion uses it to make divinations, and tell the future and provide answers to their existential questions. So, while the design form of that object inspired the design of my composition. The utilitarian and spiritual content inspired the message of the work I called "Divinity".

Outside of the museum space, there were social upheavals going on in the United States, racial tensions and police killings of black people were going on. you know, in a way I felt that what this object was telling is that if only a nation at crossroad recognizes or remembers that we're all embraced by arm of divinity, we could find healing and cease the hate that's tearing us apart both physically and spiritually.

Victor Ekpuk, Prophet

Ewan: Yes, this is beautiful … Could you could you explain *A Shrine to Knowledge, A Shrine of Wisdom*?

Victor: A friend of mine Zak Ové, a Black British artist, invited me to present work in an exhibition he curated in London called, GET UP, STAND UP NOW. He brought together Black and African artists and creatives in the U.K. and other diaspora to celebrate the artistic excellence and cultural contributions in the West. It was big, ambitious exhibition, I heard that it was one of the most attended art events at Somerset house maybe in memory.

I created a space/shrine to knowledge, a womb of archival, present and future knowledge. Where energy/data surrounds you, you can subliminally assimilate knowledge from the ether or read physical books about black and African creativity and history. I think of it as a very futuristic space of being. And within that installation was my metal sculpture, called *The Philosopher*. The furniture that viewers sat in the space was a collaborative design with Yinka Ilori, the brilliant British designer.

Victor Ekpuk, Lipstick Queen

Ewan: Your use of colour. Did you, think about it a long time or do you get precise measured, colour? How do you arrive at your colour choices?

Victor: In my pursuit for simplicity and minimalism in (my) work, even though … Yes, sometimes it doesn't appear to be so, because of the dense backgrounds in some of my compositions. I have tended to emphasis the line over colors, I approach form by reducing it to its essence through drawing. My use of color also follows this concept, color is used as a support for the drawing rather than the lines giving structure to color. To achieve this, I decided many years ago to reduce my palate to two to three colors. What is also, what is important to me is really how to apply the design of the composition to counterbalance not having that much colour.

Blue and red seems to be colors that I unconsciously gravitate to, after black. For *Shrine To Knowledge*, I wanted a specific blue, one of purest ultramarine that I absolutely adore, It's called, well, I call it the Moroccan blue. I believe that that is its origin. If you go to Morocco, you see a lot of uses of it. The French colonized it name and named it Yves Klein or Majorelle blue, but really the original Blue is Moroccan. It's a very luminous blue

I found a company in Britain that mixes it. And ordered it from them.

The quality of that blue is it is luminous and almost mystical, I wanted to create and atmosphere of a sacred space in my installation that resonates with our psychic senses, something about blue does that. It may explain why they are found on African ritual objects.

As I stood back incognito and watched people interact with the space, it was amazing to see the reactions and emotions, mostly I noticed some reverence like being in a place of worship. I smiled because I felt I had achieved my aim for that installation.

Ewan: It's a very sequestered feeling and it makes the viewer kind of want to join in in your thoughts. As the viewer, as is claimed by Umberto Eco, always brings their own thoughts, and their own unwinding processes and variations, paralleling the work at hand. We could say daydreaming alongside art is a normal participation in it. The addition of people being able to sit down in moveable stools in the space. That's really welcoming. intention in your work?

Victor: Well, the intention was to have an interactive art work where you actually come in and stay and live within the art, to be merged with it, spend time, sit, read. Just meditate, feel what you feel. That was the intention. To have, you know, art that engulfs you. You become part of the experience, really. Every object in that space, the books, including the movable stools were part of the composition. The stools were a collaborative design with Yinka Ilori who designed much of the look of the exhibition.

If you notice in the photographs of the installation before people came into it, the design is symmetrical, red top stools surrounding a green round table. But photos after the viewers have left the room shows the red stools have been moved around different to point in the space with the green table still in the center, this, in itself looked like the viewers have unknowingly participated in recomposing the composition, I enjoyed that unplanned outcome a lot.

Ewan: The viewer gets to become part of your painting whether they know it or not?

Victor: Yes.

Ewan: Do you write poetry, by the way?

Victor: I don't write it enough to say that I do. But I guess, maybe my work, is also poetry. I remember some time ago, back in Nigeria I was invited to contribute poetry for publication, I submitted a letter size page filled with my drawing, and that was my contribution to the book of poetry. I write the sort of poetry that is felt rather than read.

Ewan: Did you like the writing of Christopher Okigbo?

Victor: I have read some of Okigbo's writings. I was introduced to his collection of poems through the illustrations of the artist Obiora Udechukwu. In that illustrated volume, the marriage of artistic lines and poetic lines were sublime encounter for me. The was the light bulb moment that defined my artistic direction. It illuminated for me the of power lines, of drawing. Udechwukwu's use of Nsibidi signs and Uli forms put in perspective the whole artistic philosophy of looking inwards that I was taught by my professors at University of Ife, it gave me something I could latch my imagination onto, something that was rooted to my ethnic and family identity.

So yes. He brought out that. When I saw him, the way that he used lines and the way that he used symbols in some of the illustrations isn't popular (well known) here. That this is how I should be exploring my own work. And I started to, do it more closely. And I'm still, you know, works like that really brought me to into falling in love with drawing, falling in love with the use of lines and what it could do.

Ewan: Okigbo died in 67 or 68 in battle?

Victor: He took up arms to defend the Biafran cause and was killed in the war.

Ewan: Yes, I mean, you know, it's a bit of a sideline thing. But Christopher Okigbo. He was very well read in the classics. As you know, and I really I really admire his work.

Victor: I love his work, too. *Paths of Thunder* is prophetic.

> *Do you have to fight that war?*
> *Do you have to strap*
> *Assault riffles*
> *And pebbles of bullets?*
> *There are men and women*
> *Trained to fight that war,*
> *You are a town crier.*
>
> *Begone apprentice,*
> *I left my gong and stick*
> *At the sacred grotto*
> *Of Mother Idoto*
> *For you and your ilk*
> *For generations of town criers.*
>   —Christopher Okigbo.

Ewan: The large work in Bahrain. Could you explain that piece? It's kind of monumental in size.

Victor: The work at international headquarter of Bank ABC (Arab Bank Corporation) in Bahrain, continues my exploration of drawing lines in three dimensions, I am grateful for the opportunity to have realized this one in a monumental scale.

After a several days of several sketches, agonizing over concept and design for this project. I decided that the honest approach to this project was to focus on community in which the work will be situated. This was a welcome opportunity to research Bahraini culture, history and the people.

The layers of centuries old cultures and histories were very fascinating. The graphic systems of the Dilmun civilization spoke directly to my interest in ancient writing systems and knowledge. The result of my research started a question in my head: How do you capture the essence of a people whose history is long and culture layered in centuries of civilizations?

My answer to that question was, "look to their faces and try to catch the essence of their memory."

My impression of Bahrainis wrapping themselves in their traditional attires, is that of a people who are proud of their identity and heritage. The lines of the folds of the burka and kufiya around the faces of the wearers defined that essential identity for me and I followed those lines to the core of their portrait.

I title the piece *The Face*. It is the result of the eureka moment from my pondering. It is a portrait of Bahraini people. An attempt to articulate a people's heritage, culture, history and beauty.

I am told that the piece in Bahrain is the largest outdoor sculpture in the country.

When Bank ABC reached out to me by email and invite me to submit a proposal to the open call along with other Bahraini artists, I didn't know what to make of it. The Middle East is not where I would have even considered for public commission, I also had only a faint idea of where Bahrain was. I said yes nevertheless. On my enquiry as how, the company came to consider my work, I was told that after seeing my sculpture in a gallery in New York city, The CEO of the bank asked his people to reach out to me and extend invitation to present a proposal. The remarks of the CEO Dr. Khaled, was very heartwarming: "After reflecting on our 40-year journey as the Bahrain banking industry celebrates its 100 years this month, and to commemorate the renovation of our HQ Building, we commissioned Victor to create this unique and majestic art piece that cleverly connects our heritage and future aspirations."

Ewan: It's very beautiful. It's huge, too.

Victor: Thank you. You know, they wanted a monument piece. It has since become an iconic landmark in the country, from what I hear, it is the largest sculpture in the country. It is made of stainless steel, painted stainless steel.

Ewan: And the choice of red is?

Victor: The red nods to the red in national flag of the Kingdom Bahrain, it is their national colour. I wanted that to be something that identifies them and something they can gravitate to. And I was really, pleased when *The Gulf Weekly*, an important regional newspaper dubbed it in bold headline: 'The Face of Bahrain'.

Ewan: That's a nice moment.

Viktor Mitic

Spectral Confederation; Forms;
Coloured Dreams, Visual Music:
The Rain Paintings

This painting, *Spectral Confederation* by Viktor Mitic, a re-imagining of the Confederate battle flag, is a playfully suggested improvement, and is no doubt, emotionally charged. The original flag came into use by the southern rebel states in the American civil war in December 1861 as a battle flag due to the confusing similarities between the official confederate flag "The Stars and Bars" and the union north's flag of the United States. Since then, it has become a symbol of a number of things, including, the mythic racist Confederacy that would never be.

Artist Viktor Mitic painted it upside-down on an Ikea curtain, and in timely fashion, changed the colors of the stars to resemble the rainbow pattern of the LGBT community flag (alluding to a week earlier in June 2015, when same sex marriage was declared legal in the United States). He finished the painting by carefully shooting bullets from live ammunition along both sides of the white borders of the St. Andrews Cross in blue that forms an X through the centre of the flag. The resulting painting is comically sarcastic, lighter more extroverted presence than the original flag. It is very hard to tell there are bullet holes in this work. The holes left by the bullets have an aesthetic effect that is calming when our eyes are slowed down by the circles present. There is also the performative aspect of the presence of guns and violence associated with this flag. The presence of the artist is also there.

The feeling of this painting is somewhat satirical given the high percentage of anti-LGBT legislation in many of the former Confederate states. Its poignancy is still real, especially for anyone with ancestry of former slaves who lived very difficult and painful lives. The association of this flag as the battle flag of the pro slavery rebel confederate states is extremely unacceptable to many.

Tragically, just before Mitic painted *Spectral Confederation*, a young white supremacist went into a black church in Charleston, South Carolina, and shot nine black people dead. He was seen in the media in photographs posing with the Confederate battle flag. Public outcry shortly after caused a vote to be taken in the South Carolina House of Representatives to remove the battle flag from the South Carolina statehouse.

Some have noted that some South African symbols of apartheid were taken over during Nelson Mandela's presidency and de-racified. The springbok symbol is the most controversial emblem of white apartheid rule that no longer is generally interpreted as racist by the majority of black South Africans. It is still a symbol of South Africa. This was an unexpected act of reconciliation by Mandela and the black majority government to the white minority in South Africa. This is a big ask for anything to do with the Confederate Battle flag, and feels totally unreasonable at this point. The national flag, of the Confederacy, The Stars and Bars, which forms the basis for the state flag of Georgia from 2001, seems to attract little interest or notice in the public imagination.

Interestingly, the first time the battle flag of the Confederacy was flown at the state house in Columbia, South Carolina, was in 1961 in response or symbol of resistance to racial desegregation in the U.S. south. It was a reaction to part of the Civil Rights Movement involving Racial integration, which was a major issue in the U.S. south. Brown vs Board (of Education of Topeka), which was a U.S. Supreme court decision ruling in 1954 that racial segregation in pubic schools, even if equal in quality was unconstitutional. It took years for it to be fully implemented.

The artist donated this painting to be sold to benefit the victims of the LGBT community who suffered in the 2016 Orlando nightclub shooting.

Forms

Forms, recent sculptures by Viktor Mitic, are an entirely new aesthetic turn for the artist. He is well known for creating bullet paintings of extreme controversy that resulted in threats from the public to destroy his work as well as garnering personal death threats when one of his paintings of Jesus called "Hole Jesus" was printed on the front cover of the *Toronto Sun* newspaper in 2008. If the newspaper did not state that the painting was shot with bullets from a real gun, most viewers would be unable to tell. It was the symbol of the gun that caused such a powerful reaction. It is Mitic's use of symbols both blatant, performative and subtle that charges much of his work. One of his paintings was stolen from a gallery in 2017, during the Toronto Film Festival.

This series of sculptures is a playful reworking of mistake and accident. Much of his sculptures in this series are assemblages of reworked paint drips from his studio while working on previous paintings. His process of reworking of these shapes results in proportions our imaginations can step into by associating many of these forms with animal or human like features and likenesses. This is a point the artist is inviting us to be aware of, namely that our minds unconsciously and consciously are hardwired to try to decipher and connotatively relate to our environments. He makes this process into art.

One large sculpture is balanced to hang from the ceiling and move using a quiet motor where even the exact speed of rotation is carefully taken into consideration to be in balance with the work. These sculptures are very heavy and their sense of volume is filled out in an unexpected way from the flat planes of the aluminum shapes in surprise perceptions of space.

The surfaces of the sculptures painted with car paint nod to our times' obsession with the automobile.

So many of the shapes look mathematical especially in their approximations to French curves with similarities to the Golden Ratio that has been used in so much art and architecture and perhaps most famously featuring in the design of the Chartres Cathedral. *Lyric Neutrino Star* is a good example of this intuitive relationship in both proportions and its use of optical distortion in respect to volume which curiously has some similarity to some of Evan Penny's figurative work.

Coloured Dreams, Visual Music:
The Rain Paintings

The "Rain" paintings of Viktor Mitic are a kind of "aleatory art" in which natural rain is the constant companion of the artist as he creates mostly non-figurative pieces. He achieves remarkable results when he is working outside with his canvases on the ground under the random presence of natural rain, thunderstorms and even hail. It is as if several senses are at work, creating startling and calming effects from this inspired method. There are feelings of an almost lunar calm together with the muted immanence of solar violence in the segregated warmer colours in many of these paintings. This is an intense inner mythic-like world he has constructed that complements and includes nature. Here he paints with a sense of consumed intensity where even acid rain, like smog sunsets, can add to the final work. The more than sixty paintings cover a large range of emotional landscapes. Bright reds and oranges are swallowed by colder blues, grays and greens. Shapes are distilled to masses of dense forms in larger diaphanous washes of colder and sometimes warmer areas of surrounding chromatic space.

There is a strong suggestion of synaesthesia with sound and colour in these paintings, as if a visual music present in their composition lifts them to a multi-sensory expression. Hearing colour is an old idea. It has been described by many artists in the twentieth century, most famously by the so-called father of abstract painting, Wassily Kandinsky. He discovered his synaesthesia while attending Wagner's opera *Lohengrin* in Moscow. He said: "I saw all my colours in spirit, before my eyes. Wild almost crazy lines were sketched in front of me." In his publication in 1911 entitled *Concerning the Spiritual in Art*, he wrote: "When [blue] sinks almost to black, it echoes a grief that is hardly human. When it rises towards white ... its appeal to humans grows weaker and more distant." Another artist affected by synaesthesia was the twentieth-century composer Olivier Messiaen. He wrote: "When I hear music, I see in the mind's eye colours which move with the music. This is not imagination, nor is it a psychic phenomenon. It is an inward reality."

Earlier, Plato famously wrote about harmony and tone in relation to art, though synaesthesia as we understand it was first described by the philosopher John Locke in 1690. He mentioned "a studious blind man" who claimed to see scarlet when he would hear certain sounds of a trumpet. This now well-known phenomenon was a matter of much conjecture in the late nineteenth and early twentieth centuries, and only recently have neuroscientists been able to prove the idea of "seeing sound." How much of the population can do this is uncertain. It may be that we all can unconsciously relate to colour in some way our waking minds have no knowledge of.

Whatever the case may eventually prove to be, these rain paintings of Viktor Mitic have an immediate effect that seems to reach far more than one sense alone. They are immediately engrossing, and the imagination of the viewer is pulled in to wander in these inner landscapes he has created.

For example, there is a lunar landscape feel to the abstract painting *M0043*. Its slate blue colours and muted cold and opposing reds are covered over with transparent washes of blues which soften the warmth of the reds to make them a complementing cold. One corner of the rounded red diamond shape which has the appearance of a covered autumn leaf is showing through its cool red a small warm patch of red. This lifts our eyes for a moment to the top of the painting using the entire vertical space and creating considerable movement. To the lower right of this is a weaker red rectangular shape in front of four subtle greenish-hued paint strokes. One of these, which resembles the red shape above the line separating the shapes below, comprises the whole spectrum of all the colours in the painting. An almost human face or mask is discernible as if it were in a cloud just above the line cut off, creating a numinous presence. The surface of the painting is a rough evenly-pocked canvas skin.

Much aleatory art has been created in attempts to separate itself from mimicking nature (in terms of representing its objects and its patterns). This fictive impulse is old. Leonardo Da Vinci even complained about it in his time. As noted earlier, he wrote that "those who practice art without order are as those who fully knowing get on a ship without a rudder and set sail." In the twentieth century, there was a flourishing of attempts at entirely random art. The culminations of this were perhaps the artists who got monkeys to run across canvasses with paint on them. Viktor Mitic's *Rain Paintings* are entirely the opposite in spirit, though he does employ random elements while attending to colour theory and aesthetic design.

Ocean No. 7

There is a controlled order to the ways in which rain affects these canvases. It is an ordered chaos far from Da Vinci's complaint. There is an ordered sense to the way Viktor Mitic consciously uses rain to give the colours a consistent interrelation of part to part and as a whole in their coldness and warmth. He also uses it with shades of white in unexpected lightening of washes. The lightest in colour of these when manipulated by rain suggests diaphanous craters of white. In the centre of the city of Toronto there are days acid rain can affect the colours, giving them stronger reactions to each other which are very different from the effects he gets from similar rain conditions in more rural areas. The use of reds, blues and greens has an almost otherworldly feel, as if they were images relayed from a faraway planet.

The result of rain as it is incorporated in this series of paintings gives an aesthetic tone similar to the emotional state of being when we are around natural rain, in the sense that the feeling of the inner introspective concentration associated with rain is apparent when viewing many of the paintings. That this inner feeling is expressed outwardly on these canvases is interesting as well as pleasing. It is this world of two things that (Umberto Eco claims) we inhabit when we are contemplating art. We work through an inner landscape while interacting with art and ourselves at the same time that we are half conscious at the altar of art. This is the usual state of affairs for our imaginations, and Mitic addresses this dichotomy with timely intuition.

Viktor Mitic is relentless in experimenting with new ways of approaching and creating art. He is classically western in his restless search for something new. New expressions, new ways of looking at iconic and traditional images are coupled with new ways of painting and looking at the creative process. He goes past taboos with his use of religious iconography and current sacred images. The ubiquitous presence of guns he turns into tools for creation art in his bullet paintings. And now the life-giving essence of rain is celebrated in paint. Not just as in the past in so many paintings of raining landscapes, but rain landscapes themselves. These paintings have the quality of being viewed with a kind of pleasing intensity as if waking from moments of imagination (in front of them) to find we were dreaming.

Mitic is an extremely versatile artist. He is an excellent draftsman. He has an architectural sense of design with a subtle sensitivity to colour and its theory. Kandinsky, describing what an artist should bring to the creation of abstract art, wrote:

> Of all the arts, abstract painting is the most difficult. It demands that you know how to draw well, that you have a heightened sensitivity for composition and for colors, and that you be a true poet. This last is essential.

Viktor Mitic has these qualities, and implies that he brings to his *Rain Paintings* aesthetic mirrors of painted dreams when he says: "Sometimes paintings paint themselves."

Architecture &
Poetry of madness

—*The Soviet Embassy in Ulaanbaatar
& strange life of Vladimir Azarov*

Russian Embassy Ulaanbaatar 1970

Architect Vladimir Azarov grew up in a labour camp with his parents from the age of 5. He recounts his strange life in his autobiographical writing, and suggests part of his later success as an architect may have been from guilt by the authorities in the 1960s for those who were unfairly punished by growing up in Stalinist era labour camps. He said that he sometimes wondered if it was a paying back for his father's treatment of being sent to a labour camp with his family, for listening for a few minutes to Radio America with a neighbour. His most well known building is the Russian Embassy in Ulaanbaatar, Mongolia, completed in 1970.

Azarov upon retiring from being a successful architect in Moscow, moved to Canada. It was there that he started recounting and publishing his personal stories which became a poetic witnessing of totalitarianism. Growing up in a labour camp in Kazakstan, it was hidden from him that his family was in political exile. At the time, he thought "people must always be coming to these difficult Soviet work colonies in the east from all parts of the country." This gave him an unrealistic optimism which helped him to overcome many of the challenges of his life at the time and to find his own way to live in that artificial world.

"One must dare to be happy," Azarov says of this perceived blindness. He said he cannot remember who other than Gertrude Stein said this but, it became his philosophy.

These poems written in the form of short stories are able to bring past moments and lost times to life. Azarov does this with what appears as effortless ease. His ability to bring immediacy of experience and the poignancy of loss into the reader's current imagination in bittersweet poetic renderings often makes the listener or reader wait on the edge of his or her own imagination for the next turn in the story.

For me it is his ability to find small moments of poetic arrest, like half-hidden living things in scarified landscapes, which interrupt some of the bleak and desperate times he has lived through.

He writes in his poem "Broken Pastries" of his experiences of sharing a cave for a few weeks one summer with a free running goat, a dog and an old woman who survived an extended time in the Soviet Gulag. He presents the pain and suffering of others around him with respect and a kind of aesthetic compassion that is almost always a pleasure to read. Making art from memory is not as easy to do as is commonly thought. There is a frequent tendency to underestimate the difficulty of this simple style that requires what Tolstoy called a "sincerity" of expression.

Azarov now writes variations on famous works of literature interweaving new possible readings and interpretations. But it is when he writes about the common sufferings of people he has known, often from the intolerance and paranoia of the Soviet regime, that he is at his best. As in "Rag Doll" where his feeling for the prisoner of war and very skinny German soldier who was gratuitously beaten up and injured by the poet's father while the family was in exile in the camp in 1945 is still a vibrant memory. It is as though Azarov has made friends with exile and he is able to relate to its sorrow as a kind of comfort.

These events and times that seem so remote are not so remote and their terrifying import could easily be recycled in our future history.

The Community of Jesus, Grenville Christian College

The Art of Deception

Isolation is that impasse into which men are driven when the political sphere of their lives, where they act together in the pursuit of a common concern, is destroyed ... While isolation concerns only the political realm of life, loneliness concerns human life as a whole ... totalitarian domination as a form of government is new in that it is not content with this isolation and destroys private life as well. It bases itself on loneliness, on the experience of not belonging to the world at all, which is among the most radical and desperate experiences.
—Hannah Arendt, *The Origins of Totalitarianism.* (477)

1.

Despite their ground in human creativity and freedom, it has long been known that music, art, and poetry are central to the construction of forms of social order and control. Plato banished them from his ideal Republic. In the case of the controversial The Community of Jesus cult, their art, music and poetry programs were crucial pillars in the construction and maintenance of what former members' accounts reveal to be a totalitarian micro-community. The music and art programs especially have served as legitimating fronts for this charismatic Christian group, whose top leadership live lives of luxury while many of its lower level members live very modestly, with many giving much of their money to the group, while taking vows of loyalty and obedience to the leaders for life.

My experience as a young child starting at age eight and including forced extended stays through most of my teenaged years, as well living at its close affiliate, Grenville Christian College, a boarding school near Brockville, Ontario, for three years, was one of extreme isolation, violence and loneliness.

An Ontario Superior Court ruled in 2020 that Grenville Christian College, whose staff were members of and lived by the values and practices of the Community of Jesus in Orleans, Massachusetts, engaged in decades of abuse of students between 1973-1997. Its former headmaster Charles Farnsworth claimed that the staff of the school were members of the Community of Jesus. It closed in 2007.

Judge Janet Leiper, in her decision issued February 23rd 2020, in a class-action suit against Grenville Christian College, stated:

I have concluded that the evidence of maltreatment and the varieties of abuse perpetrated on students' bodies and minds in the name of the (Community of Jesus) values of submission and obedience was class-wide and decades-wide.

According to one of the representative plaintiffs, the Community of Jesus was not named as a defendant due to issues of jurisdiction. The Community of Jesus founders Cay Andersen and Judy Sorensen were linked to the school's methods of discipline and religious practices during the trial. The more than 70-page ruling explained the Community's involvement both spiritual and financial to Grenville. Charles Farnsworth's son Donald testified that the school gave about 100,000 dollars every year to the Community of Jesus. Cay Andersen and Judy Sorensen were on the board of the school.

Grenville Christian College

Over the past twenty years
Grenville Christian College has been
greatly blessed by the Community of
Jesus, which is located on Cape Cod
in Massachusetts. The truth and the
life which comes from their lives
lived in obedience to God brings this
same truth and life to the Faculty,
staff and students at the College here.
   Music has long been part of the

From a Grenville Christian College yearbook 1990s. Bottom left is
"Mother" Betty of the Community of Jesus, beside the Community of
Jesus choir.

The school was originally started in 1969 when the
dignified old Catholic building of St. Mary's College
(built in 1918) was leased and later purchased, by couples,
Al and Mary Haig and Charles and Betty Farnsworth as
a Berean Christian School. The Bereans, based in Texas,
were on the conservative fringes of American Christianity

of their day. By 1973, the school was already in debt and needed repair. The headmaster, Al Haig, invited his long-time friends, lay preachers and faith-healers Cay Andersen and Judy Sorensen to the school. These were the same people who had proven their holiness by praying for and healing his family dog of distemper a number of years earlier. Now under self-styled titles, "Mother" Cay Andersen and "Mother" Judy Sorensen came to speak to staff about the Community's way of life and its extreme religious beliefs. They had originally planned to stay a few days but ended up staying much longer, teaching daily about how to use light sessions, and how to deploy their version of tough love on students. According to Al Haig's autobiography, which he published with The Community of Jesus press, the staff prepared to go on regular retreats to the Community of Jesus, and became members along with the school leaders. Haig even wrote about one of his early public light-session by the Mothers in his book. It reads as a kind of submission to their authority on Grenville. Here is his account of one of their speeches:

> Judy spoke first. "God has given us a scripture first to describe what He is about to do here. *The axe is laid to the root of the trees.* This college is like a twisted tree that must be hewn to its very roots, in order that a tall, straight fruit-bearing tree can grow in its place.
>
> "Your methods, your way of doing things, your philosophy of education, your ways of dealing with young people, your opinions, your plans have failed. It's time to start all over again—this time, God's way."
> —Al Haig, Headmaster, 1980.

Their way of life, centred around light-sessions, obedience and death to self, was brought into the school and
with staff going frequently to retreats at the Community
of Jesus, it soon became their way of life. They bought a
house in the Community and were always represented
there. One affidavit by a former member recalls Charles
Farnsworth in a phrase I also remember him saying on
several different occasions, that the Community of Jesus
is his spiritual home.

Staff members paid (or tithed) 10% of their salaries
to the community. The school also gave a substantial
amount of money to the community to pay for retreats,
as well as buying a house in the Community compound
in Rock Harbor, Orleans, Massachusetts. One former
senior member and witness, is on record saying: "I am
now ashamed to admit it, but I was brought into the
room as muscle to get Al Haig to submit to the mothers
bidding on an issue at Grenville."

The Community of Jesus Compound Cape Cod, 2019

The Community's attorney said in a statement via email to the Cape Cod Times:

> The most important facts speak for themselves: the plaintiffs in a Canadian court case alleged 13 years ago that as many as 45 years ago, individuals at an institution not in any way, shape or form run or directed by the Community of Jesus, in another location in another country that is hundreds of miles away from Cape Cod, engaged in wrongful conduct against them.
>
> There was no claim filed against the Community of Jesus. There was no finding by the Court that the Community of Jesus had engaged in wrongdoing. What there was was the Canadian plaintiffs' claim that certain individuals in Canada took what they regarded as the 'idea' of certain individuals who 45 years ago had been involved with the Community and that those purported 'ideas' were in some fashion partially 'responsible' for the misconduct of staff at the Canadian school.

And yet, "Mother Betty," then leader of the Community, wrote a letter dated in 2000 to staff at the school, that "the vows (to the Community of Jesus) taken by many at Grenville"—including, swearing obedience to the group's leaders—still applied.

A brief history of the Community of Jesus is in order, to understand where they got their mind-controlling "Light-sessions" which were used to subjugate adults and used especially mercilessly on young children in their compound and then later, on unsuspecting young boarding students at Grenville Christian College from 1973-1997.

The Community of Jesus has its origins in another controversial also entirely self-founded sect begun in Darmstadt, Germany in 1947 in the ashes of World War II, called The Evangelical Sisterhood of Mary. This group has also been frequently accused of being a both a cult and a business by former members as well as many others. There have been scathing popular and academic accounts of their practices.

The founders of the Community of Jesus, Cay Andersen and Judy Sorensen, visited the Evangelical Sisterhood compound in Germany for several extended visits during the late 1960s, and later invited the self-styled mothers from Germany to Rock Harbor in Orleans, Massachusetts to help them set up their own sect in the U.S. They originally called their fledging group "The Little Sisters of Mary." This was in 1968-69. Judy Sorensen, later to become self-styled "Mother" Judy of the Community of Jesus (which was incorporated in 1970), started having a sexual affair with one of the

German Sisters of Mary. This prompted the German self-styled "Mother" Basilea to summon all the women back to their compound in Darmstadt, Germany for stern correction.

Leaders Cay and Judy with child in 1980s

Community of Jesus marching band c. 1980s

One of the primary methods of control in the Evangelical Sisterhood of Mary was "Lichtgemeinshaften" meetings, or as the Germans translated into English for the Americans, "Light-sessions". This is an allegedly Christianized ritual variation of a method of mind control technique with similarities to one used in Germany during the Second World War, and in another loose variation, during the early Soviet Union under the name *Critio ic Critto.*

Light-sessions originally were an evangelical and extreme attempt to live a Christian life according to the Bible passage in the New Testament, 1 John 1.6-7:

> If we claim to be sharing in his life while we walk in the dark, our words and our lives are a lie; but if we walk in the light as he himself is in the light, then we share together a common life, and we are being cleansed from every sin by the blood of Jesus his Son.

The Christianized element is the scriptural "living in the light," by pointing out each other's sins, but in a very confrontational and methodically proven and highly-processed way. This is done where the person being Light-sessioned is not allowed to speak and several other members are "wolf-packing" (as former C of J elite member David Manuel states) them in the most hurtful and psychologically abusive way. In these meetings those being Light-sessioned are often forced to admit to previous sins or emotional wounds (which are often imaginary or entirely made up) these are then used to get the person being "Light-sessioned" to submit to authority.

This is almost always followed up by a collective "love bombing"; this love-bombing after submission is very important, as the emotionally raw Light-sessioned individual is vulnerable to attestations of care and love at this moment. The person Light-sessioned is told how much they are loved by the same people who were just emotionally abusing them in Light-sessions. They are told that the people in the outside world don't have real friends like their friends Light-sessioning them in the Community of Jesus. I do not know of a single counselling professional taking part in any of these meetings. This was entirely amateur and done as the leading members felt inspired by "the spirit" to do in the moment.

New members would be slowly and gently eased into this lifestyle, until they were hooked. Then their light-sessions would be much harsher and in line with how the Community actually lives. Many members seemed to become emotionally addicted to these light-sessions. This proven and very effective method was the model for authoritarian control and submission at the Community of Jesus. One former teacher at Grenville and Community of Jesus member said in an interview with the news program W5 that "this was our way of life." There are some differences to The Evangelical Sisterhood of Mary in Darmstadt, Germany, which I will go into later. At the Community of Jesus Light-sessions could come at any time, they were unrelenting. In recent years the Community of Jesus has dropped the use of the word Light-session, but former members who have left recently say they are still going on with the same level of intensity that they were when they were the subject of criticism by *Chronicle*, a Boston Television news documentary in 1993. I was addressed with the ferocity and intensity of a light-session (that I remember so well) by a long term Community member (I knew as a child there) with witnesses present while visiting the compound within the last two years. It was clear to me from this experience, and from extensive interviewing of many members who have recently left, that this practice of Light-sessions still goes on, even if the term is no longer used.

When I was a child at the Community of Jesus starting at age eight, the Light-sessions were terrifying, and often accompanied by violence and always with the threat of violence. Public confessions of guilt (of often unintelligible things to a child) were in a kind of imitative Catholic confession style but in public, and the adults would be playing the roles of the god-inspired priests, by granting the forgiveness of god after punishments to the children for the most minor of infractions, and when there were none, which was often, some were made up. There was a kind of follow the leader imitation of how the leaders presented themselves. The authoritarian nature of the sect made following orders from the leaders like following god. This was all made worse by most children being separated from their parents, as was the general practice. I was forbidden to speak with my parents. I was 8 years old. (The children of the very wealthy were the only children I remember being allowed to live with their parents when I was there.)

The patterns of authoritarian control at the Evangelical Sisterhood of Mary were copied at the Community of Jesus and later Grenville, and were more extreme due to the personality issues of leaders Cay and Judy. A former member of the Evangelical Sisterhood, Cay's own son Peter Andersen, stated that Mother Basilea told Cay and Judy that they should not run a monastic community with children. Basilea also disapproved of Light-sessions on children. Cay and Judy disagreed.

It was on the basis of the very harsh, mind control 'Light-sessions' lifestyle that the Community of Jesus was organized and controlled. Its leaders managed to lead lives of luxury with a private plane and an estate in Bermuda, while so many of those of the low ranks and young children suffered.

The two 'mothers' from Germany had given themselves the names "Mother Basilea" and "Mother Martyria". They were obsessed with German guilt over the Second World War and they wanted to employ the same techniques used by Germans during the war but for the good of pointing out German guilt.

Mother Basilea had a PhD in psychology and seems to have used her knowledge to considerable effect. The website of the Evangelical Sisterhood of Mary states: "God commissioned our two spiritual mothers to build a chapel where he would receive honour and worship. As confirmation they received the following scripture: 'Let them make me a sanctuary that I may dwell among them.'" (Exodus 25:8).

Here are excerpts from a piece originally written in German in 2007 (under the title *Eine ehemalige Marien-schwester erzählt ihre Geschichte*) by Charlene Andersen about light-sessions during her 14 years as a member of the Evangelical Sisterhood of Mary in Darmstadt. (She left in 1999):

> … and Mother Basilea took over the lead to the community and also the lead of the 'Lichtgemeinschaften'. On the basis of Johannes 1.9." (If we confess our sins, he is faithful and just and will forgive us our sins and purify us from all unrighteousness.)
>
> These 'Lichtgemeinschaften' meetings were meant to cleanse the sisters from all evils. *(Lichtgemeinschaften means Licht = light, Gemeinschaften means communities— so it means 'Communities of Light')*
>
> And this is how the 'Lichtgemeinschaften' were carried out: one sister after another had to confess which of their own words and deeds had harmed the community. While she (one sister) was standing there, everybody, who found something sinful in the standing sister, was invited to speak …

The 'Lichtgemeinschaften' meeting took hours and it happened often that the sisters who were criticized a lot broke down, cried and condemned themselves … During these meetings it was not allowed to justify oneself. One had to act quietly and subservient and to humiliate oneself …

I think the terrors of these meetings I have never overcome. Instead of creating harmony and healing within the community these meetings created, to my view, mistrust and fear … My description will be eventually a warning for the subtle power of spiritual seduction.

The ones among you who have never been a member of a sect will have challenges to understand what I am talking about …

(She uses the German word *Sekte*, but it arguably could also be translated as cult—it appears to be a much stronger word than the English "sect").

Peter Andersen, the son of Cay Andersen stated.

Both Mothers from Germany spent months at Rock Harbor (*Community of Jesus*) in the late 1960s training Cay and Judy in Light-sessions, or "monastic" discipline. I think Cay and Judy brutalized it to an extent they didn't practice in Germany and Farnsworth took it to a new level at Grenville … The institutional foundations were, for sure, rooted in the practices of that order in Germany. And to an extent, in the Third Reich.

According to Peter Andersen, Cay said: "We're going to do this 'community thing' better. We can do better than these people."

Several former members have written accounts of their time in the Evangelical Sisterhood. Their philosophy at first, appears to be a kind of sin-drenched make-it-up-as-you-go kind of rag-tag thing, seeming much closer to extreme American puritanical evangelical Protestantism (Pentecostal), rather than contemporaneous mainstream European protestant traditions. After a closer look it is much darker which I will go into later.

Here are some excerpts of accounts of mind controlling light-sessions by former members of the Evangelical Sisterhood of Mary:

> Caught up in the intensity of the experience, almost no one asks about its theological foundations. The Sisters claim that it is not their "commission" to expound theology, nor are they a Bible college. The intellect is not held in high regard although the proclamation sounds logical. Religious feelings and experiences are also not the aim. The objective is simply to help Christians to a deeper discipleship and love for Jesus. The way to achieve that is through repentance and contrition.

> As long as I was a guest, repentance was a liberating experience of confession and the pronouncement of forgiveness in the name of Jesus Christ. However, as a guest you do not learn the practical meaning of repentance within the Sisterhood. Most guests only hear that the Sisters are attending a "Fellowship in the Light."

Fellowships in the Light provide the framework for the concrete expression of repentance. It is here that sins that have affected other members of the community are openly confessed and forgiveness for them is proclaimed. The sisterly ministry of admonishing one another over unrecognized guilt is also performed here. It is the site where God drills into the hearts of the Sisters until tears of contrition flow. This is the source of the reconciliation that is the secret of Canaan.

The similarities of Light-sessions at the Evangelical Sisterhood, The Community of Jesus and Grenville are astounding. Cay and Judy copied almost exactly the way the Evangelical Sisterhood was run and set up their own version with the German Sisters' help and oversight. This pattern is fundamental to understanding these groups.

Just like at the Community of Jesus and Grenville, members, students, and children dreaded these light-sessions. Though after sustained periods of time enduring them, for some people they became very highly addictive.

Another a former member of the Sisterhood writes:

Mother Basilea knew that we shuddered at the thought: "We know that—understandably—many fear Fellowships in the Light. However, in spite of the fear, one can still thank Jesus for them: Even if it hurts me and I find it difficult I want to love Fellowships in the Light because I know that the truth makes me free."

What are the consequences of the Fellowship in the Light for Sister X? Nervous breakdown?

According to Mother Basilea it serves towards spiritual healing and not a breakdown:

> We become spiritually healthy when we are broken; this is precisely the opposite of what our intellect tells us. We think: "If I had to experience something like that I will be spiritual broken." But the reality is that I become spiritually whole because it is God's action in my life. 13th July 1983.
>
> Mother Basilea teaches that no Sister of Mary will be spared such an experience. God will choose a time to deal with her through His chosen instruments. She encounters Him as the God of Wrath who is completely holy and recognises through the encounter that she is but a 'vessel of sin.' God deals the sinner a 'blow of death' to annihilate her 'selfhood.'

At the Community of Jesus Light-sessions were often even more savage as has been publically stated by many ex members. They could happen at any time, and for any reason. They were usually off the cuff and sudden, seemingly coming out of nowhere. Although they could come at any moment, there were also very organized and scheduled "light-sessions". These light-sessions were so emotionally upsetting as a young child being ganged up on by several adults that children often would over time, lose a sense of their inner selves, as I did. They were very frequent and unrelenting. I watched as members would become hooked on them, often saying that they felt close to god during them.

At Grenville the staff who were all members of the Community of Jesus (when I was there) sometimes scheduled them as "Light-groups" with each other and with non resident members of the Community, following the Community of Jesus practice. The travesty is that at Grenville the mostly emotionally damaged staff freely exercised them on unsuspecting students who would have no previous understanding of the practice and experience it for what it was: severely abusive mind control. The students being very young would have no way of fighting back and would usually just internalize it.

Over time they became highly addictive to many of the members especially those with troubled backgrounds, which appeared to be most members.

Peter, Cay Andersen's son, stated this about Light--sessions:

> But almost every strong thing, say a beautiful sunset can release endorphins. well, these light-sessions, they're so bad and they're so painful, your body produces endorphins to counteract that, and you think it's a spiritual experience and that god is closer to you because of it.

I have found this to be one of the most accurate descriptions of the emotional links between perceived spiritual experience and Light-sessions. These light-sessions can, especially over time, make people feel like they are close to God. My mother was a very devout member of the Community of Jesus. She described being Light-sessioned at the Community of Jesus as being very close to God, as an experience of God (in extensive recorded interviews toward the end of her life).

The following poem by a Community member seems to describe a light-session that members know so well. The psychological intensity of them over time can bring people to doubt themselves on the deepest emotional level. As mentioned before, it is a very effective control technique, especially when inflicted so frequently over many years. I have noticed that heavily Light-sessioned people would have a hollowed out social presentation, especially children. (This is never present with the leadership who seem to always be the same people, and usually very wealthy):

> Upon your return
> I thought while you were gone upon the things
> you'd said. Those words still clear, so pure, with wings
> and flames descended to my heart and burned,
> and there renewed that offering fire of sin,
> which finds its fuel in excess there within.
> Those words were more than words, and how I yearned.
> —A Brother

Respected professor Dr. Ronald M. Enroth wrote a chapter about the Community of Jesus in his well-known book—*Churches that abuse* (Zondervan: 1992). (http://www.reveal.org/development/Churches_that_Abuse.pdf)

Here are some excerpts of what he wrote about the Community of Jesus:

> Discipline resulting from the infraction of rules or 'failure to keep with the program,' as well as 'spiritual disciplines' imposed for one's spiritual betterment, have

been reported by former members of the Community of Jesus, a controversial charismatic Christian group located in the Rock Harbor section of Orleans, Massachusetts, on Cape Cod. The Community of Jesus (COJ) exemplifies commitment to self-sacrifice and a semi-monastic life-style in the context of what The Christian Century referred to as 'tasteful affluence.' The COJ accommodates resident members, associate members, and non-resident members, as well as the many middle and upper-middle-class Christians who journey to the Cape each year to participate in retreats sponsored by the organization. Some of the evangelical notables who are associated with the Community include David Manuel, Peter Marshall, Jr., William Kanaga, who is Chairman of the Advisory Board of the New York firm Arthur Young, and at least one member of the Rockefeller family.

Two laypersons, Cay Andersen and Judy Sorensen, founded the Community around 1970 (Mrs. Andersen died several years ago). They soon became affectionately known as 'Mother Cay' and 'Mother Judy,' and were at the center of the controversy that has swirled about the organization in recent years. In addition to what one churchman called its 'lack of ecclesiology,' the COJ has been accused of promoting a 'theology of control' that focuses on attitudinal sins like jealousy, rebellion, wilfulness, haughtiness, and idolatry. Critics and former members have argued that the Community has shifted toward an unbalanced, unbiblical, and highly structured program resulting in some people being abused emotionally and spiritually. There have also been reports of some forms of physical abuse. Media accounts, including an extensive article in Boston magazine, have aroused suspicions. These have been denounced by the CoJ leadership.

Interestingly, Enroth did not comment on the children and how damaging it must be for them. As a child, it was emotionally crushing to be isolated whenever I was there from ages 8-16. I often thought of suicide as did other children. Among other things, there were times I had my head repeatedly smashed on the floor by adult members and was forced to eat my own vomit to 'break my spirit.' I was nine years old when this started. I was not allowed to speak with my parents who were living in another house. I later as an adult two years ago, confronted a former leading Brother and a leading Sister in their gift shop about this and received a conflicted near apology. Here is a small part of Brother Peter's response:

> (I held my recorder up in front of me. I said I was a writer and I repeatedly said they did not have to speak. I also spoke of severe abuse to children at both the Community of Jesus and Grenville)

> Ewan Whyte [00:00:00]: When I was a child I was here at the Community of Jesus. As a small child, at age 10, I was forced to eat my own vomit by (adult members) Wally Swidrack and Anne Swidrack in the house that you called Judea. And it was utterly devastating experience, and when I think of the children … It kept on going on—light sessions …

Ewan Whyte [00:00:29] Constant light sessions, beatings ...

Ewan Whyte [00:00:31] I was pushed down the stairs by Wally Swidrack and I had damaged vertebrae to my neck. I was taken, it was on Uncle Ben's way, I was taken around to see a doctor and we aren't certain if he even had medical training.

Brother Peter said he was not in a place to speak for the Community. He then said this, the second of two qualified responses or near apologies)

Ewan Whyte [00:03:16]: You don't have to say anything.

Brother Peter [00:03:19]: I'm not challenging anything you're saying, I'm not countering it, I'm not accusing you of anything that's wrong that you're saying. I'm very, very sorry if that ever happened. It's not for me to apologize, but obviously it was an extremely damaging and extremely unfortunate, terrible thing and I don't know what else to say. I mean, I'm, I'm grieved that that happened.

Sister Chris [00:03:43]: And we pray for your healing. We certainly understand.

An intense series of events followed this, including the cult's leadership trying to get the local police to charge me with disorderly conduct which they refused to do. It was my impression that the police were on the

Community's side, or at least afraid of their influence. The Community pushed for a hearing before a magistrate. The magistrate clearly knew the Community leadership involved in perusing this and had me charged for disorderly conduct. My lawyer was outraged and said this is ignoring the law. He was very surprised by the events. The judge later sided with me and threw the charges out. The recording was determined to be mine. This shows the character of the leadership of the Community of Jesus.

* * *

The CoJ tried to find affiliation with some mainstream churches but there were no takers. They have found a number of enablers who would sometimes separate when they would see how the children were treated. Enroth notes:

> Since 1982, several presbyteries have initiated studies and critical assessments of the COJ, including the Presbytery of Boston and the Presbytery of Genesee Valley (NY). These studies were undertaken because of the heavy involvement of members and pastors of certain Presbyterian churches in various COJ programs and retreats. In a report dated June 1987, the Synod of the Northeast concluded, among other things, that 'There is some evidence that in the use of authority, some of the disciplines and practices of the Community of Jesus have been appropriated by individuals in less than helpful ways. The Agency [Synod Vocation Agency] is particularly conscious of the authoritarian nature of the Community of Jesus.

Despite many groups researching the abuse at the CoJ, it has managed to find some admirers. One was a former Ontario Anglican bishop who ordained Grenville Headmasters, and Community of Jesus members, Al Haig and Charles Farnsworth as Anglican priests, despite the fact that Farnsworth had no university training. During the ceremony, "Mother" Cay and "Mother" Judy sat in the audience and CoJ senior member Arthur Lane gave the sermon. Documents claim Bishop Hill visited the CoJ a number of times, as an official visitor. He was frequently at Grenville, and statements claim he was even an oblate or non-resident member of the CoJ.

Enroth again quoting ex member Don on the CoJ:

> While the leaders continue to say that they don't force anybody to do anything, there is such moral persuasion and such peer pressure that there's no question that you would do whatever you were expected to do. The alternative would be anything ranging from a beating to being sent away from the Community, which meant, separation from Jesus.
>
> Like members of other abusive groups, Don was led to believe that he was joining an elite team. We were often told that there was no place in the world like the Community, that it was special. Don believes that many people who join the Community have problems beforehand, or are spiritually immature, and therefore vulnerable to manipulation. "People who were there all had reasons for joining. Perhaps life was not going well for them, or they were searching for something they

couldn't find. By clever manipulation, the leadership convinced them that they could find it at the Community. I was a new Christian, and they convinced me that I would best find Jesus at the Community. To leave the Community was to get out of God's will."

Don pointed out that no negative criticism of the Community was tolerated, a distinguishing feature of most totalitarian groups. "No one dared to say anything negative of any kind. I was actually afraid of being beaten up physically by members of the Community if I got out of line."

Don was an adult there and at least, would have seen that parents were separated from the children. He may have not realized the extent of how violent both psychologically and physically it was for children there. Children who are still growing and developing are incredibly vulnerable to this kind of treatment. It is carried with them for the rest of their lives. It is surprising how many former members leave and seem to forget about the children still in there. This is a constant disappointment.

2.

At Grenville, I knew I could not be friends with any of the other children. Grenville intensely followed the CoJ's practice of Light-sessions as well as creating networks and hierarchies of informants: we were all exhorted to tell on one another for any infraction, supposedly to help our 'friends' see the light. There was a considerable incentive to tattle—tattlers would be rewarded with praise, and most importantly, would avoid being in the hot-seat, at least for that day. It was pretty much impossible to have friends, and there certainly was little trust among the staff children.

We were not to speak to our parents because our parents, we were told, would treat us as idols, loving us more than Jesus. Idolatry was a major thing with Community members. Cay and Judy brought it up in most of their many "teaching tapes" that Grenville staff and staff kids were supposed to listen to all the time. Parents wouldn't be firm in punishing us, and they wouldn't be firm in making us follow the true way of Christ that this Community of Jesus had revealed. I had already learned at the compound that complaining to my mother or another adult was the surest way to be punished.

In a "retreat" tape from the early 80s—"Idolatry, Anger and Lust"—the "Mothers," accompanied by the famous evangelist and Christian author Peter Marshall Jr., use Luke 14: "If anyone comes to me and does not hate his own father and mother …" to justify their understanding of idolatry:

Judy: [B]ecause I chose God over my children, they were ultimately able to choose God over themselves. […] I didn't understand it because I thought it was cruel, unloving, and neglectful, but I obeyed God anyway, whether I understood or not. […] When I was preferring them, when I was spoiling them, when I was turning my back on their sin …

Cay: They were a mess!

Peter: Yeah.

Judy: … [B]ecause you control them through your idolatry, and they want your idolatry, they want your love, your money, your acceptance, your forgiveness, your leniency, but they hate you for not demanding of them what God wants you to demand of them. […] You are building up a kingdom of hate and rejection and loneliness for yourself when you do to your children what's by nature our desire to do with them."

Peter: We see this problem over and over in counselling. […] It's the other parent who coddled them, who tried to make it up to them.

This exchange between the leaders shows the Community of Jesus and Grenville's attitude to parent-child and student-child relationships in their care and influence. This attitude was vigorously upheld at Grenville. This was also a way in which adults dealt with each other at the Community and Grenville. Community of Jesus member and second in charge at Grenville, Joan Childs, said, "If the people in charge told us to do something, we did it" (1:02, part one of 4, In the Name of God, W5, 2016)

THE COMMUNITY OF JESUS

BETTY C. PUGSLEY, ADDRESS

Advent
November 30, 1997

Dear Family,

This Advent I have again on my heart – prayer. In a way Advent begins for us a new cycle of the church year, a new year of anamnesis – the acts of our Lord and the humans who surrounded Him. I have always wrestled over the scriptural direction "to pray without ceasing." Wiser minds than ours direct our legalistic, scientific understanding towards its meaning. It is an attitude of heart. We are not born with this attitude, but its opposite. Our attitudes of heart are only of self!

Our community is called, as others have been in history, to seek God in community. Here we are to learn to love aright. Here each of us is important. God uses us in each others' lives to work this "new testament" - new concept - new covenant of love. Our vows *rate* as for this continuing work, and prayer causes desire, appetite for this work to happen. Without this burning fuel, called prayer, our appetites will follow their natural beat. Self-fulfilling work - books - food - sleep - TV - sex - fun - trips, etc., will take an ungodly place and become what we live for instead of where God intended them, and as he intended them, for us.

"But God has called us here to an active life," you say.

"Don't I know it!" I wholeheartedly agree. So is most of the rest of the world. We live in the most active, talkative, traveled century. We have the task to be taught of him how to bring this *praying heart* into all that we do. Will we want it? NO! Our ego loves to survey all *we* have done.

It avoids the reality of *who we are*. Therefore we must set our wills as disciplined warriors to run this race that is set before us.

Love,

Mother Betty

7\30\92

David Manuel - does not need to worry himself with the salvation of the world. Those who are put in his path and those who are given the community or Paraclete Press as places to receive help and guidance, these souls are enough. I want to make it clear that obedience is the individual heart is what I am after. My Son asks each of His children to allow His will be the grounding and guiding mercy of their soul and this is the case also with David. He does not have to look outside of the work before him for the comfort of accomplishment, but look to what he is called to do and it is there that he will find the strength and mercy of God. It is simple, it just needs to be obeyed.

That is all.

Letter of unknown authorship to David Manuel

STAFF PHOTO BY GORDON E. CALDWELL

The entranceway to the Community of Jesus complex in Rock Harbor, Orleans.

se

>me for-
1embers
casional
essed, a
1ore con-
here.
eek, for-
attern of
abuse at
-middle-
at Rock
ts to the

y is spo-
l. But for
al abuse
   said the
Anglican
nity five
's navel-

mmunity
as far as

d the lar-
"Oh, the

emotional damage.... You can never feel good about yourself." I
said he was emotionally damaged
during his five-year stay at the
Community.

And two pastoral counselors on
Cape Cod — the Rev. James Wood,
pastor of the Chatham Baptist
Church, and the Rev. Dr. Ellendale
Hoffman, a psychologist and Episco-
pal priest in Falmouth — said they
have seen emotional damage in former Community members.

On Friday, former members of the

Community met and spoke with
members of news media to describe
alleged abuses in the organization.
Incidents of slapping, kicking and
other physical assaults were described by the former members.

Other former members have told
of the emotional abuse that they received at the Community, and told of
how they have been shunned by people in their families who remain inside the Community.

See THE 'GUILT', Page 9

The Cape Cod Times from the 1980s. This was long before the significance
of the situation for children was realized by the public.

The following are some very brief excerpts with
commentary explaining parts of this long article:

"*In a written response Saturday, The Community la-
belled as untrue the former members' allegations of abuse.
'We do not know of any physical, emotional or threat of
physical abuse,' said the statement, which was issued by
Barbara B. Manuel, The Community's executive secretary.*"

John Sorensen, co-founder "Mother" Judy's own
son said:

"*They have a very sophisticated system of peer pressure and psychological pressure.*" Sorensen said that the

community operates on the presumption that they can look at you or me, see what our problem is and presume they can fix it. It's a frightening use of the Gospel of love, which I thought was about love." Such an approach is unfair, Sorensen said, because it does not take into account the problems of the counsellors and is unfair to the counselled. "They have no say, not really, unless they really raise some hell and get out of there," he said. "It abuses people's sense of worth."

The real significant issue here is once again, these are adults talking about adults, not about young impressionable and entirely defenseless children. In these articles (of which there are a considerable number), you can read a significant amount into the fact that children are almost entirely absent from the discussion. If so many adults were deeply damaged, you can imagine how much more damaging these experiences would be for young children. Very many former members as well as students at Grenville still suffer as adults decades later today.

Rev. and Counsellor Wood said later on in the article:

"It saddens me to see people, who because they are so eager to do God's will, are taken advantage of," Wood said. "The Bible says that there is one God and one mediator between God and Men, the man Christ Jesus," Wood said. "People coming out of the Community seem to be encouraged to rely on other mediators, rather than on Jesus … Rather than hearing God's will for themselves, (Community members) are encouraged to find out God's will from their superiors."

Continuing the point of control here, Grenville's Headmaster Charles Farnsworth's dictated letter to the defense of Community leaders, Cay and Judy, shows the depth of the links between them.

"People who have worked with the Community have praised the organization. They include the Rev. Charles R. Farnsworth, headmaster of Grenville Christian College." ... *"In a letter dictated over the phone Saturday to Barbara B. Manuel, the Community's executive secretary, Farnsworth said that the school's association with the Community has brought it "a sense of peace and order, as well as a unity for the corporate life of a community and private school."* Farnsworth later says Grenville's staff regularly attends retreats and spends time for "spiritual refreshment" at the Community of Jesus.

Most notable are these lines from Farnsworth (yet again) linking the leadership of Grenville with The Community of Jesus and its leadership:

"Last year the school's board of directors expanded from four members to seven, and asked that Mrs. Andersen and Mrs. Sorensen serve on the board, and they accepted," Farnsworth said. *"It is difficult to find words that express what these people mean to us all."*

From the left, Lewis Sheen, Charles Farnsworth of Grenville performing as a leading priest at "Mother" Cay's funeral, Arthur Lane, Hal Helms, "Mother" Judy Sorensen, Bill Sorensen, October, 1988.

3.

There was a kind of twisting of facts that became inter-woven with how life was lived. We see an example in the following article self-published by the Community called 'Choose Life' written by Hal Helms, then a senior member in the Community of Jesus (around 1988, the time Betty Pugsley aka Elizabeth Patterson was moving toward taking over leadership of the CoJ).

He writes:

Jesus warned that there is a broad road leading to death, and it is a crowded way. He said the way to life is narrow and the gate is straight. Robert Frost said it like this:
I shall be telling this with a sigh
Somewhere ages and ages hence,

Two roads diverge in a wood, and I—
Took the one less traveled by,
And that has made all the difference.

Helms ends the piece here. This shows he clearly does not understand the poem or its deliberate ambiguities and humour. Helms has taken this poem out of context and twisted it to fit his clumsy procrustean bluster.

Frost wrote this poem in 1915, during the First World War as a joke with meaning, for his friend, the British poet Edward Thomas. The two were regularly going on walks together to discuss their writing. This poem makes statements, then doubles back, just like the walks of Frost and Thomas. The opening, as has been commented on many times, is like the beginning of a fairy tale, that could be from Lange or the Grimm brothers. The playfulness of fable is misunderstood here, as is connotation for denotation. The playful lines of the poem state that the paths were worn really about the same and this is not a choice of a road to death and life. It is (among other things) an internal meditation on indecision and our sense of relating to it in terms of our unconscious or as in fairy tales/parables.

These previous lines in the same poem help to fill out a deeper and conflicting meaning, and as Robert Frost used to joke, a moment of wisdom:

Then took the other, as just as fair,
And having perhaps the better claim,
Because it was grassy and wanted wear,
Though as for that the passing there

Had worn them really about the same.
And both that morning equally lay
In leaves no step had trodden black.

The actual meaning of the poem is the opposite of how Helms attempts to present it. This twisting of the meaning to fit particular whims is typical of my experience of the leadership in the Community of Jesus to this very day.

This sect presents itself as an arts-oriented Benedictine community (despite not being Benedictine). Its current leader, self-styled "Mother" Betty, was (unknown to most) actually its amateur choirmaster for several years, under the name Elizabeth Patterson.

Their choir, though competent, is still an amateur choir, and not everyone has seen them to be as good as they seem to see and present themselves. This choir presents as a legitimizing force for the Community but it surely must be heavily financed to have such reach, with so many self-published recordings. Ellen Pfeiffer, writing in a now completely-expunged (from the internet) article in the *Boston Globe* in 1999:

> [I]n the Bach Motet "Singet dem Herr nein nues Lied" the chorus seemed out of its depth. Bach's complicated counterpoint is challenging for even a professional chorus and the group could not keep the threads of discourse clear.

In another now-expunged article (also no longer available online) in the *Boston Globe* around the same time, years after Betty's husband and former Community of Jesus choirmaster left the sect after being caught sexually abusing boys, Betty (Elizabeth Patterson) tells Ellen Pfeiffer that she was still consulting with Richard Pugsley Sr. about their music program:

> My husband is not longer directly involved with the choir, because he's branched off into chant (another activity of the community is the publication of chant recordings through the Paraclete Press.) He left me with the whole nine yards of the choir, but this was a joint decision. There is still a lot of breaking information about chant, and it is helpful to have an expert consultant!

To be clear, this was over a decade after he was caught sexually abusing several of the boys at the Community of Jesus and yet was consulting with his wife and others for their music program long after he had moved to England. It appears that no charges were ever laid, though some of the boys' families were paid off. If this doesn't boggle the mind, former members say Rick Pugsley was allowed back for a visit to the Community in 2007 or 2008 where he was welcomed. Members reported Betty and Richard Jr. went to her house in New Hampshire at that time.

Self-styled "Mother" Betty, it turns out, is a poet as well. Her poem is included in the 1988 Community of Jesus' self-published publication in a poetry anthology section in honour of Mother Cay. An excerpt of Betty's poem reads:

Now with inner eyes we strain to catch faint celestial
colors:
Perfect …
  Pure …
    Hinting of solid essence.
Now with inner ears we strain to hear unheard sounds
…
  Singing not marked by soul or strife, but selfless praise
and adoration.
    Now the feet of our mind walk with a pair of scarred
feet …
Taking companionship through:
    Sunsets …
      Swans …
        Flower gardens …
          Hedgerows no known before …
You are there …
    Growing …
   Seeing …
    Dancing …
    Running …

This is the kind of writing we would expect from
almost any average aspiring teenaged poet. It is the fact
that this is not a young person, but self-styled Mother
Betty, an adult around fifty years old at the time, with
public pretentions to "high" art, and soon to be the
leader of this highly authoritarian sect that this is worth
noting.

The tired line "not marked by soul or strife" is not the kind of poetic effort we expect from someone who portrays themselves as a major artist as self-styled Mother Betty under the name of Elizabeth Patterson does. To the reader, it comes off as a beginner's work grasping for a poetic thought or phrase that sounds like it is reaching for something profound, but by its vague unspecific grasping, finds itself beneath the realm of Hallmark cards. The following listing off of activities followed by ellipses speaks for itself. This is not any better or worse than beginner poetry. Pretty much anyone can write this kind of verse. Expecting any innocent passer by to read it and take it as "high art" with a straight face is another thing.

Perhaps, it is the performing of the music of Bach and Palestrina that may make someone think they are also a creator of art on that level.

Here is a selection of poem excerpts of Community of Jesus poets. Self published in their glossy magazines for sale, and to be mailed to their non-resident members and supporters around that time:

I want to be very different

I want to be very different,
from who I am today,
It really, impressed me,
all because of Mother Cay.
Life has so much more meaning,
than it ever had before …
    —Brother David

Window to Heaven

Windows brought her pleasure
in her busy life with us.
A peaceful moment to treasure—
no bother and no fuss …
      —Sheryle Snure

Full Sails

We are but fragile boats, O lord,
Upon the sea of life,
Tossed to and fro by woesome waves
Of selfishness and strife …
      —Buzz Elmer

In Romsey Abbey

Loft, flowing, fleeting song,
Scripture, chorus, tolling long
Beating color, grace and blessing …
      —A Brother

Fight the Good Fight

Across the fields the tromping soldiers go,
with naught but bloody bayonets to show
their conquering spirits sought the heavenly tide
to ride, and finding power beneath their hands
to stab and kill and leave for wandering bands,
they've done their work and left their murdered pride …
      —A Brother

The reader is going to have to decide if these excerpts are the artistically elevated work of an elite group of individuals chosen by God before the foundation of the world to be part of a select group that cannot be matched (as I witnessed and many former members attest was the way the Community saw and presented itself).

It is hard for me to see anything exceptional or special about this group in terms of artistic merit or cultural understanding. Rather, it is clear that as a general group, they are not specially cultured. I have never met a member of the Community of Jesus or Grenville staff that had a significantly informed understanding or knowledge of history, art, or literature (1) or culture (outside a specialized and rather esoteric Christian revisionist standpoint). Even the children of the founders acknowledge that the founders were not generally, culturally interested people. They have one formidable enabler, Timothy Verdon an American Monsignor who regularly performs mass in the cathedral of Florence. I briefly visited him in Italy in 2019 and here are some excerpts of the conversation we had. The first is on their art.

> **Ewan** [00:22:32]: On the other side, what do you think of their (CoJ) art, I mean, do you like their art? Their artists?

> **Verdon** [00:22:36]: That's a very different kind of question. What does that say?

> **Ewan** [00:22:41]: I mean well I think it's fascinating. You know (the Gothic era) Abbot Suger (of Saint-Denis), "the

mind of man rises to God through the senses." I think their art is a little bit on the kitsch side? Their taste?

Verdon [00:22:52]: Well one or two of them are all right. Others I don't especially care for. I don't organize art exhibits for them.

Earlier we discussed abuse allegations at The Community of Jesus and Grenville. Here are excerpts of what he had to say:

Verdon [00:07:10]: Right, well they wanted my, two of my texts for the Paraclete press. But I never heard any of these things, so I'm not able to evaluate them. My question to you would be are any of the people presently active in the Community at Orleans among those who have been accused of sexual abuses?

Ewan [00:07:50] You're talking about Richard Pugsley Senior, is what you're saying. Richard Pugsley Senior is in, he's in Cambridge, England, and he was—.

Verdon [00:07:57]: I've never met him.

Verdon [00:08:02]: Is the one who was?

Ewan [00:08:02]: He's one of the ones. There's several children in that case. I grew up partially as a child at the Community of Jesus. They made me eat my own vomit on several occasions. I have this stuff signed off on.

Verdon [00:08:21]: And you were there, your parents?

Ewan [00:08:23]: I was an eight-year-old child, and they were making me eat my own vomit.

Another speaker [00:08:28] They'd remove children.

Ewan [00:08:29]: And they removed children from their parents and you would have to live in separate houses, but incidentally actually, they've copied everything from the Evangelical Sisterhood of Mary which is a German cult in Darmstadt. They copied everything. But the light session originally was called Lichtgemeinschaften—communities of light. And that was the origins of a light session but ultimately its totalitarian origins go further back in German history.

...Verdon [00:14:24]: The only real connection I seem to make to what you're saying [inaudible] is [inaudible] occasions when I was [inaudible] at Orleans. They did try to explain this system where more than one family is in a house and sometimes the children go and live with other families [inaudible] others explain it in a different way. And um [inaudible]. They went out of their way to have me meet the young people. Interesting and a bit surprising, I interpreted it as their way of allowing me to be assured that these young people were not being brainwashed, and indeed, they seemed, [inaudible] divided into, two groups, very young kids and adolescents and all seemed to be extremely well socialized, and balanced and much more adult than kids their age usually are. [inaudible] I'm having difficulty coping with the things you say.

He later said:

Verdon [00:18:58]: I have seen them (The CoJ) in not only in action in their own place, but in context here and indeed I introduced them to very important people in the Church in Italy, all of whom remain deeply impressed by them, and so what you call manipulation comes across to us here as real sincerity.

The Community self-published an article about their leaders getting an audience with the Pope in 1988, and giving him a gift of art created by the Sisters and Brothers in their sect. The title of the article is "All Roads lead to …" In it the connection that the Community had for its leaders to get an audience with the Pope must have been considerable. Their influence has been significant over the years locally and to a certain extent beyond. They even got their leaders into the White House for a chat during the Reagan era.

The meeting with the Pope is problematic, as after so much press about abuse in their sect there were no alarms in the leadership of the Catholic church at the time:

[W]hen it became clear that such a meeting was being looked on favourably by officials in the United States who have responsibility for such things, plans began to be made to follow through, including the preparation of suitable gifts for the Holy Father when and if the audience should take place… they carried with them sketches of the gift which would be made by the Sisters and Brothers of the Community, and answer questions about the nature of the Community of Jesus, so that

the Pope's representative would get a clearer idea of who
and what we are.

That the Catholic Church with all its reach and
influence failed to find out about the abuse is not believ-
able to me. Surely someone must have chosen to look
the other way. The fact that this meeting was facilitated
shows their influence:

> The largest (and heaviest) was the stained glass triptych, a
> three panelled work with an image of the Blessed Virgin
> Mary, with the words in Polish which are especially mean-
> ingful to the Pope. The side panels had words in Latin:
> "I will strengthen you, I will help you." (Isa 41:10) Carved
> on the bottom frame are the words: "Totus Tuus"—"I am
> all yours," the Pope's personal motto ... the frame was
> fashioned and carved by the Brothers of the Community
> as their contribution to the gift. In addition the group
> took with them three leather bound volumes: David du
> Plessis' last book, *Simple and Profound*, and Betty and
> Rick Pugsley's book *The Sound Eternal* (the story of the
> development of Gregorian chant here), and a three-in-
> one volume of the living library series. *Imitation of Christ,
> Confessions of Saint Augustine* and *Lead Kindly light.*

This was a big event for them and the pictures of
them posing with the Pope was an incredible photo op.
It lifted their credibility to its highest level yet. There
was no mention of the children in this Community.
I wonder if any of the officials even thought to ask? Cay
and Judy with Betty Pugsley along with only the very

wealthy and elite of this sect are in the photos in St. Peter's square in Rome, Italy.

Let us hear from a former sister of over 20 years, one of the people who actually designed this art and worked on it for a many hours. Her words are very different from what outsiders might expect.

Once I was asked to help design a piece of stained glass to present to the Pope. Yes, our clergy were going to Rome for an audience with Pope John the XXIII, the Ecumenical one. Another Sister and I designed the piece. The brothers did the woodwork. I will speak for myself. I was "put on silence" before this task was given. Can I ask you how one communicates rationally with another human being when one can not speak? … Many times, they informed me that they did not want to hear what I had to say. … I remember the torture of not being able to communicate. I also remember that Thanksgiving Day came during this time. I went to the meal in the Dining Room all the Sisters were assembled, I ate my meal in silence and then left. Continuing to work on the stained-glass piece. We had to explain to the ministers who would transport it to Rome via airplane, then Taxi. They had to be instructed how to put this triptych together, because it was transported in three separate panels. … The beauty that was exhibited in that elaborate piece of artwork with the Pope's motto carved into the wood and metal numes of Gregorian chant running through the panels, certainly hid the pain and anguish of soul of the one who did much of its creation. I'm sure the Pope never guessed.

She continues:

There appears to be a great discrepancy coming from the Community of Jesus. This discrepancy is seen clearly in their fantastic claims regarding their artwork, namely their mosaics, their so-called world-class choir, their pottery and painting and the beautiful delivery of meals to guests.

May I say there is a vast discrepancy between what they call beauty and prestige and the lives of the ones that produce this so-called beauty. Has anyone ever interviewed one of the choir members? Does anyone really know the lock and key they live under, or the disciplines imposed for the slightest infraction? Since I worked in one of the areas of art there for a good 20 years, I think I should have a voice. Your own life is under continuous scrutiny. One lives under the threat of exposure for what they call infraction, therefore one lives in fear continually. They call it obedience and actually it is a vow that one takes which is totally unbiblical. They claim love is obedience. What they mean is 'do what I say or get punished.'

The punishment could come in many forms. Imposed disciplines I would call them.

Their artwork does not whitewash the sinister way members are controlled. Certainly it cannot erase the profound, lifelong damage done to the innocent children who have the misfortune of being brought there or being born there. Can you imagine being born into this and then home-schooled on top of it? You would never know there was a real world out there. Your values would be skewed, and you would never be able to apprehend the marvellous, wonderful full beautiful love of the real God who created you.

The level of secrecy and some would say delusion that the lower ranked followers live under is remarkable. They were receiving letters about their lives from the leaders. There were significant efforts to hide from the press, that they were presenting to members letters from the Virgin Mary herself, composed specially by her for their community. This practice has been affirmed by both former staff members at Grenville and attested to by several former members of the Community of Jesus, including original letters produced by former senior member David Manuel and others.

The musical programme is the highlight, and it occurs to me that perhaps above all else, the music is a pharmakon; both a form of discipline and violence if one is a member of the choir, with the punishing hours and stern leadership. It is also the palliative for sorrows, and an incredibly effective public front.

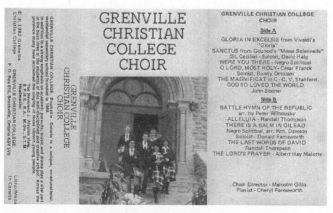

Photo of Grenville Christian College choir, cassette tape 1980s.

Notes from a noted American academic attending a concert at Community of Jesus Church of the Transfiguration in the mid 2010s:

6:45 pre-concert talk

very elderly audience of about 100 in the chapel—talk directed to their level—oohs and ahs at every surprising tidbit revealed

the church itself is astounding—Chairs, not pews—for daily office (sung by the entire community) chairs face in. Choir rehearses one hour a day—but (a child of one of the founders) said rehearsals in their day used to be 3-4 hours called arbitrarily to make people have to be ready to jump at any time.

No expense was spared in the chapel—elaborate baptismal font, huge carved bronze doors with gold inlaid brass around them—fountain outside the door—organ pipes inside shuttered boxes the full length of both sides of the nave—110 ranks now, headed to 150.

Large mosaic of Jesus at front of the church I find a little strange and frightening. A looming, almost demonic face of Jesus hovering overhead (maybe I'm projecting here; I was told it was based on Christ Pentacrator, which you can see from the darker right side), arms open with lines coming down to the floor that almost look like leashes, while obedient sheep process up to the top and out the door of light—those doors are duplicated below with opaque glass—the theme is obviously the "light" of Christ, (perhaps symbolic of the "light sessions"); the angels on the sides also have wings with eyeballs down the center.

The art is strangely old fashioned in a dated and an epigonic way, that seems almost 1970s style kitsch, though this is relatively recent work. The overall effect of so much busy art (made by non members, apparently to the Community's designs and standards) in one place, presents for me an alienated sense of what this group is. The art of the Community tells a strange story and it is clear from their choice and arrangement of art that they are trying too hard to present a particular persona to the public. The result is an appearance that is fitting for such a group. It is still a kind of warning to the unsuspecting, that something may be quite off with this group.

Some of the Community members are claimed by former members to be painted into the faces of the figures on sides of the church. This antique custom may seem atavistic in our time. It is strange to see the obviously Black figures from the bible painted as if they were only slightly Black. This was commented on as well by Black American academic who accompanied me on visit on one day. The question was asked if there were any current Black members of the Community. We were told not at this time. We never saw a single Black person even visiting. It was eerie to see this art painted in the old fashioned "white-washed" kind of way, with only lots of white people around. "Even the Black people are presented in as close to white people as possible way."

The Christ figure in the centre of the church is one of alarm to me. It appears to me as an aggressive eerie-cartoon Christ, not a gentle Christ of forgiveness. It suits the Community well. For me, it is a cartoon-kitsch style representation so fitting to the kind of authoritarian sect that commissioned it.

As well, some of the mosaic designs are credited to leadership members of the group. I did not see designs credited to any lower ranking members.

Notes from an academic visitor from just a few years ago:

> Upon meeting a couple who said they were non-resident (or oblate) members of the group for about 10 years. They claimed to come mostly to see the choir.
>
> I asked plenty of leading questions to see what their awareness of the cult-like aspects of the community were (like: "Do the families each have their own house?" "Do the kids go to school outside the community or to college?" Answer: some do, some don't)—but they seemed to be well-off members of the community without a clue about the darker aspects of the past.

On their concert and music performances the professor had this to say:

> The chanting was antiphonal between the men and the women—a very nice, smooth, light sound, and fairly fluid and comfortable with the antiphons from the *Graduale Triplex*, which they all sing from. But the psalm verses themselves were very machinelike with no accentuation—explanatory material about the music program at COJ talks about using the Latin because it matches the chant, and the book (someone) showed me (*Triplex*) had English penciled in throughout. But it didn't look like there was time for awareness of the text (though they did observe the mid-verse pause). They are trained to genuflect if they make a mistake.

The singers came on from the side very quietly, the men in tuxes and the women in long gold dresses —the older ones with fancy red Chinese jackets over the dresses; they started with Bach's motet "Komm, Jesu, komm"—the opening text translates "Come, Jesus, my body is weary—I am becoming ever weaker ..."—they sang with a light, soft, bright, breathy sound and equivalent smiles on their faces—precise and in tune but without any expression or inflection resembling the music's relation to the text. I thought to myself, how are they going to sing the Vaughan Williams "Dona Nobis Pacem" (a big piece with orchestra) with a sound like that? I found out soon in some early Mozart selections that they do *forte* too, when asked. A very firm, ringing sound. They all take voice lessons and theory lessons from the conductor (Oberlin and NEC) or his assistant (SMU and Eastman).

The women sang the Poulenc *Litanies for the Black Virgin* flawlessly in terms of tuning and blend, but with little inflection. The conductor was very business-like —everything clear and in its place—but almost deliberately without any visible emotion, mouthing the words, or facial expression of any kind, even in the big moments of the Vaughan Williams. Finally at the beginning of the last big passage his face warmed and the faces of all the singers responded instantly. Up until then, they had been as expressionless (but precise) as his conducting, very still, fairly natural looking, but with little animation, movement, or apparent effort of any kind ... The whole performance had a weird feel to it—it felt as though a performance hadn't really "happened"—there was no drama, no spontaneity, no engagement—but the audience was appropriately awed ...

The strangest thing happened at the end of the concert: The conductor extended the silence at the end, as is typical, but in this case rather static. The audience then began to applaud, and soon stood up slowly for the obligatory standing ovation after such a work. But then when the conductor and soloists left the stage, the clapping just quickly petered out before even one curtain call. Even with such a spectacular piece having been just been performed with a high level of accuracy, there was no energy in the room—no sense that what should have been a riveting performance of a penetrating piece of music had just happened … the energy just left the room suddenly, and everyone just sort of looked at each other as if to say: "well that was excellent, wasn't it?—I guess it's time to go."

4.

There are many different views on how the Community is out of step with mainline Christian denominations. Here is one of the more interesting assessments from my extensive interviews. This is one opinion from a very educated person with experiences of the Community of Jesus as well as lengthy contact with some of the founder's children:

> My interpretation of (one of the founders children's) assessment of Cay/Judy motivation: A confluence of genetically-based mental illness on the part of the founders (Cay's multiple personality disorder with extreme narcissism and Judy's severe bi-polar disorder) forged

into a pathological psycho-sexual relationship with exceptionally charismatic leadership giftedness (intuitive perception, persuasion, confidence) creating an environmentally-based mental illness among the followers, which then becomes permanent through fear and physiological changes over time (as documented in research for cognitive therapy.

A former senior member said the children now are not even allowed to go to public school (though several members claimed that this was up to the parents, and that not all were homeschooled). When one of the founders' children was going to the public school in Orleans, they had to wear special clothing and were not allowed to invite other children to the Community or participate in any social or extra-curricular activities. Now the isolation for the children seems to be almost total (if this is true).

For the mass, most of the sisters and brothers left, which was strange; other community members came in, include two women with 6-7 young girls (around 8-10 years old I think) who looked quite shell-shocked and sad. I asked a community member about participation, as was told that was usual—people had other things to do—which I thought was strange in a community where liturgy was apparently so central—this would seem to be the main service of the week—it's not like they live far away—and Mother Betty again was not there (she "had meetings since very early in the morning" ... on Sunday?) The organist played the hymns very fast—the community was almost reciting the words while being very light on the tunes because there wasn't enough time to really sing them. The sermon was pedantic and seemed to be from someone who is probably a high-level "enforcer" under Mother Betty. The parable of the sower was the text, but the theme was related more to a quote from François de Fenelon (a 17th C. French bishop) on the cover of the leaflet, which I found quite saddening when I first sat down:

It is hard to believe that a loving God could allow us to suffer. Does it please him? Couldn't he make us good without making us miserable? Certainly he could. God can do anything. Our hearts are in his hands. But he does not choose to spare us sorrow.

One visitor to the Community of Jesus associated the group with a passage in Dostoyevsky's The *Brothers Karamazov*:

The Inquisitor's words to Jesus, [as imagined by Ivan]: Too, too well will they know the value of complete submission! And until men know that, they will be unhappy. Who is most to blame for their not knowing it?—speak! Who scattered the flock and sent it astray on unknown paths? But the flock will come together again and will submit once more, and then it will be once for all. Then we shall give them the quiet humble happiness of weak creatures such as they are by nature. Oh, we shall persuade them at last not to be proud, for Thou didst lift them up and thereby taught them to be proud. We shall show them that they are weak, that they are only pitiful children, but that childlike happiness is the sweetest of all. They will become timid and will look to us and huddle close to us in fear, as chicks to the hen. They will marvel at us and will be awe-stricken before us, and will be proud at our being so powerful and clever that we have been able to subdue such a turbulent flock of thousands of millions. They will tremble impotently before our wrath, their minds will grow fearful, they will be quick to shed tears like women and children, but they will be just as ready at a sign from us to pass to laughter and rejoicing, to happy mirth and childish song. Yes, we shall set them to work, but in their leisure hours we shall make their life like a child's game, with children's songs and innocent dance. Oh, we shall allow them even sin, they are weak and helpless, and they will love us like children because we allow them to sin. We shall tell them that every sin will be expiated, if it is done with our permission, that we allow them to sin because we love them, and the punishment for these sins we take upon ourselves. And we shall take it upon ourselves, and they will adore us as their saviours who have taken on themselves their sins before God. And they will have no secrets from us. We shall allow or forbid them to live with their wives and mistresses, to have or not to have children according to whether they have been obedient or disobedient—and they will submit to us gladly and cheerfully. The most painful secrets of their conscience, all, all they will bring to us, and we shall have an answer for all. And they will be glad to believe our answer, for it will save them from the great anxiety and terrible agony they endure at present in making a free decision for themselves.

It is interesting to note that much of their relationship with the outside world appears to be almost entirely inner-directed through their self-legitimizing arts programs. There appears to be no mission to the poor or disadvantaged and their Christian publishing program, Paraclete Press which also self-publishes their choir's recordings, appears to be, a for profit venture. Their buildings are excessively grandiose and out of place for the area. Clearly, they are to impress outsiders.

They continue on after 50 years, and after several investigations and news programs, many news articles and many complaints from former members. The naming of the Community in the successful court case against their close affiliate Grenville has changed things. We should remember the children still inside. It seems the children have been forgotten and left to fend for themselves. We can look at the art and think this is the kitsch of an authoritarian group, or we can think of the children being groomed to make it. I was once one of these.

Acknowledgements

Some of these essays were published in the *Globe & Mail* and *Exile*, others accompanied shows at Gallery Möos, Christopher Cutts Gallery, Odin Wagner Contemporary, and Deluca Gallery.

Acknowledgement to:

Hisako Omori, Ruth Marshall, Michael Mirolla, Molly Peacock, Raza Rizvi, Kelley Baker, Scott Perry, Sean Lipsett, Patrick Georges, Big Poss, Little Poss, Mark Robertson, Mike Kirney, Bonnie Bowman, Siobhan Flannigan, Siobhan Jamison, Peter Cresswell, Art Szombathy, Mark Achbar, Laurie Kwasnik, Steve Davies, Evelyn K, Eve K, Peter Jermyn, Blair Walker, Bald Bruce Jones, Jason Logan, Sasha Wentges, Kurt Weider, Joe Duffy, Arthur Ulamek, Jeph Nightingale, Howard Goldstein Szombathy, and Monty Cantsin.

About the Author

Ewan Whyte is a writer and translator. He has written for the *Globe & Mail* and *The Literary Review of Canada*. He is the author of *Desire Lines: Essays on Art Poetry & Culture, Entrainment,* a book of poetry, and a translation of the rude ancient Roman poet Catullus.

Printed in October 2021
by Gauvin Press,
Gatineau, Québec